BOOKS BY NICK LYONS

Jones Very: Selected Poems *(editor)*
The Seasonable Angler
Fisherman's Bounty *(editor)*
Fishing Widows
The Sony Vision
Bright Rivers

NICK LYONS

Bright Rivers

CELEBRATIONS OF RIVERS
AND FLY-FISHING

A FIRESIDE BOOK
Published by Simon & Schuster Inc.
New York   London   Toronto   Sydney   Tokyo

Though some of the material in this book first appeared, in different
form and with different titles, in the various publications listed below, I
have felt no obligation to be loyal to those versions. A series of articles
does not make a book, which must find its own unities; I have let the
raw matter of those versions stew in my imagination. Combined with
much that is new, or completely rewritten, some of the sections here
originally appeared in *Fly Fisherman* (© 1976, 1977 by *Fly Fisherman*),
*Harper's, Sports Afield, Gray's Sporting Journal, Fawcett's Fishing
Journal* (© 1977 by Fawcett Publications), and *the fly fisher*. I am
grateful to the publishers of these publications for permission to reprint
this material.

Copyright © 1977 by Nick Lyons

First Fireside Edition, 1988
Published by Simon & Schuster Inc.
Simon & Schuster Building
Rockefeller Center
1230 Avenue of the Americas
New York, New York 10020
Published by arrangement with the author.
FIRESIDE and colophon are registered trademarks
of Simon & Schuster Inc.

Manufactured in the United States of America

10 9 8 7 6 5 4 3 2 1   Pbk.

Library of Congress Cataloging in Publication Data

Lyons, Nick.
  Bright rivers.

  "A Fireside Book."
  Originally published: Philadelphia : Lippincott,
1977.
    1. Fishing.   2. Trout fishing.   3. Fly-fishing.
  I. Title.
[SH441.L92   1988]   799.1'1   87-31070
ISBN 0-671-65744-5 Pbk.

For Mari,

WHO REMAINS PATIENT

CONTENTS

Bright Rivers

Gray Streets,
Bright Rivers

*Every object rightly seen unlocks a quality of
the soul.*

RALPH WALDO EMERSON

IN the evening on upper Broadway, two blocks from my
apartment, lynx-eyed women stand near the bus stop as the
buses go by, waiting. They wait patiently. Their impassive
rouged faces show only the slightest touch of expectation;
their gold high-heeled shoes glitter. Their dresses are exceed-
ingly short. One of them hums, and the sound is like a low
cacophonous motor, in perpetual motion.

A man asks, with startling politeness, "Would you be kind
enough to spare me fifty cents, sir, for a cup of coffee?" Later
I see him caterwauling, along with a young tough, eyes wild,
waving a pint bottle of Seagram's. Nothing here is quite as it
seems.

Four blocks away, only last month, an ex-cop "looking for
action" found himself dismembered by a pimp and then deposited, piecemeal, in several ash cans in front of a Chinese
laundry I once used.

On a given evening you can see:

9

The diminutive Arab who every night paces rapidly back and forth in front of the old church, talking incessantly to no one in particular; men rigged up to look like women, with bandanas and false breasts, arm in arm, leering; more lynx-eyed women, one of whom, quite tall and extraordinarily thin, reminds me of a Doberman pinscher; a few tired old men closing up their fruit stalls after working sixteen hours; some fashionable people in front of Zabar's or one of the new restaurants, who look like they've been imported, to dress up the place, from Central Casting; the bald, immie-eyed Baptist—his eyes like those little marbles we used to call steelies—his face bass-belly white, with placards and leaflets, proclaiming to all who will listen that the end of all things is surely at hand. Perhaps. Or perhaps not.

Everyone is an apparition, connected to me by eye only. Why am I always looking over my shoulder, around corners, then, to see who's tracking me or what will be? Hunted by ghosts. I want to become part of them, any one of them, to feel their pulse and know their heart, but I fail; some part of me is locked. Bill Humphrey says these people are only ahead of their time: we'll all be there soon.

And sometimes I see, in the early evening, a glimpse of sunset through the rows of stone, catch the faintest smell of salt, and even see the Hudson itself, sullied but flowing water.

I know no more than ten people among the thousands who live within two blocks of my apartment. Next door, for five years, I used to see a grizzled old fart by the name of Mr. Maggid look out of his second-story window now and then. Sometimes he would call to my sons in a high-pitched voice and throw them pieces of candy; at first I half suspected the sweets were poisoned. A year ago, another neighbor from that building came to me one night, his wife with him, and said, "Mr. Maggid is dying."

"I'm sorry to hear that," I said. I didn't know Mr. Maggid. I didn't know what to feel.

My neighbor paused, then added, "He won't leave his room. You can hear him coughing and groaning in there— it's awful—but he won't answer. The door's locked. About a week ago he told me he wanted to die in his own apartment, no matter what happened. He didn't want to die in some sterile hospital. What should I do?"

A moral decision.

Suddenly, in death, Mr. Maggid's life is linked to mine. No more casual encounters by eye; no more candy dropped thirty-five feet down, suspect, never eaten. He is no longer a stranger like that woman who collapsed on the pavement last winter; when I stooped to help her, a passing lawyer told me I'd better keep my distance—I could be held liable for her death.

What to do?

"I really don't know the man," I explain.

"You can't just let him die like that," says my neighbor's wife.

"He wants to die in his own room."

"Maybe he didn't mean it," says my neighbor.

"He meant it," I say. I have known lonely men.

"Maybe not."

"Does he have any relatives? Any real friends?"

"None." The word is absolute.

"The poor man," says the woman. "You can't let him die all alone up there. You've got to call a hospital, or the police. Maybe they can save him."

"That's the point," says my neighbor. "Maybe he's not really dying."

Finally the neighbor calls the police. On my phone. Does that make me liable? And for what? They come, three of them in blue: solid men who will know what to do. They pound on Mr. Maggid's locked door. They shout. There are a few moans, as if some inhuman creature had been walled up in a Poe story and wanted to stay there. Ten minutes later a bright white-and-red ambulance, its top lights turning and flashing, arrives; someone produces a crowbar and brings it upstairs; then I see Mr. Maggid come down the stairs he rarely used, feet first, on a stretcher, an oxygen mask held to his mouth, his eyes wide, then small, darting, then still. An hour later we learn he has died in the hospital. The next day, our neighbor describes to us Mr. Maggid's room. It has not been cleaned in more than fifteen years. Garbage was never taken out. Hundreds of pornographic magazines piled with soiled clothes in the corners and closets. Dust. Dust over everything. The landlord, who had taken legal measures to get Mr. Maggid evicted so he could jack up the rent, can't face the place and takes a year to clean it. A dour bearded guy who edits Woody Allen's movies lives there now. We never speak.

Downtown, where the game for the big green is played, I go to a meeting that lasts eight hours. After the first ten minutes, I feel the tightening in my chest. I begin to doodle; I scribble out a meaningless note and pass it to someone I know across the table, because I've seen executives in the movies do that. I look for the windows, but they're hidden behind heavy, brocaded draperies so that the air conditioning will take—anyway, we're in the back of the hotel so even if the windows were open, I'd only see the backs of other buildings. Everyone is talking with pomp and edge; I jot down Evelyn Waugh's observation, "that neurosis people mistake for energy." I drink two glasses of ice water. I speak like a good boy, when spoken to.

Suddenly I begin to sweat. I've been in this windowless room for fifteen years. I have been a juggler, flinging my several lives high and carelessly into the air, never catching them, barely feeling one as it touches my hand. Nine to five I am here; then a salt stick on the subway and five hours in the classroom; then I am the fastest ghostwriter in the East, becoming a lawyer one week, an expert on Greece the next, then an adopted girl searching for the blood link. When there is time, after midnight, I write high-toned scholarship—on Chrétien de Troyes and Thomas Nashe and William Ellery Channing and Saint Augustine—and shaggy-fish stories; or I prepare a lecture on "The Generosity of Whitman." A smorgasbord, my life. Five hours of sleep and back at 'em again, the ghost who is not what he seems, back at meetings like this one, dreaming.

I say my piece in front of all these important men as enthusiastically as I can. These are the rules of the game. Part of what I say—a few words—has to do with rivers. From my words I catch their briefest warbling sound, like the faint rush of wind among the leaves, or a rushing faucet, and when I sit down, there in the back of the hotel, with the windows covered by heavy drapes and the smoke from cigars (mine among them) thick around our heads, as strategies unfold and campaigns thicken, I see a glimpse of them, inside. Deep within me they uncoil.

Rivers.

Bright green live rivers.

The coil and swoop of them, their bright dancing riffles and their flat dimpled pools at dusk. Their changes and undulations, each different flowing inch of them. Their physics and morphology and entomology and soul. The willows and alders along their banks. A particular rock the size of an igloo. Layers of serrated slate from which rhododendron plumes like an Inca headdress, against which the current rushes, eddies. The quick turn of a yellow-bellied trout in the

lip of the current. Five trout, in loose formation, in a pellu-
cid backwater where I cannot get at them. A world. Many
worlds.

> . . . oft, in lonely rooms, and 'mid the din
> Of towns and cities . . .

as Wordsworth said in "Tintern Abbey," about a nature he
felt but never really saw,

> . . . I have owed to them
> In hours of weariness, sensations sweet,
> Felt in the blood, and felt along the heart. . . .

Yes, I owe rivers that. And more. They are something wild,
untamed—like that Montana eagle riding a thermal on extended wings, high above the Absaroka mountain pasture
flecked with purple lupine. And like the creatures in them:
quick trout with laws we can learn, sometimes, somewhat.

I do not want the qualities of my soul unlocked only by
this tense, cold, gray, noisy, gaudy, grabby place—full of
energy and neurosis and art and antiart and getting and
spending—in which that business part of my life, at this time
in my life, must of necessity be lived. I have other needs as
well. I have other parts of my soul.

Nothing in this world so enlivens my spirit and emotions
as the rivers I know. They are necessities. In their clear, swift
or slow, generous or coy waters, I regain my powers; I find
again those parts of myself that have been lost in cities. Stillness. Patience. Green thoughts. Open eyes. Attachment.
High drama. Earthiness. Wit. The Huck Finn I once was.
Gentleness. "The life of things." They are my perne within
the whirling gyre.

Just knowing they are there, and that their hatches will
come again and again according to the great natural laws, is

some consolation to carry with me on the subways and into the gray offices and out onto upper Broadway at night.

Rivers have been brought to me by my somewhat unintelligible love of fishing. From the little Catskill creek in which I gigged my first trout to the majestic rivers of the West—the Madison, the Yellowstone, the Big Hole, the Snake—fishing has been the hook. And in the pursuit of trout I have found much larger fish.

"Must you actually *fish* to enjoy rivers?" my friend the Scholar asks.

It is difficult to explain but, yes, the fish make every bit of difference. They anchor and focus my eye, rivet my ear.

And could this not be done by a trained patient lover of nature who did not carry a rod?

Perhaps it could. But fishing is *my* hinge, the "oiléd ward" that opens a few of the mysteries for me. It is so for all kinds of fishermen, I suspect, but especially so for fly-fishermen, who live closest to the seamless web of life in rivers. That shadow I am pursuing beneath the amber water is a hieroglyphic: I read its position, watch its relationship to a thousand other shadows, observe its steadiness and purpose. That shadow is a great glyph, connected to the darting swallow overhead; to that dancing cream caddis fly near the patch of alders; to the little cased caddis larva on the streambed; to the shell of the hatched stone fly on the rock; to the contours of the river, the velocity of the flow, the chemical composition and temperature of the water; to certain vegetable life called plankton that I cannot see; to the mill nine miles upstream and the reservoir into which the river flows—and, oh, a thousand other factors, fleeting and solid and telling as that shadow. Fishing makes me a student of all this—and a hunter.

Which couldn't be appreciated unless you fish?

Which mean more to me because I do. Fishing makes rivers my corrective lens; I see differently. Not only does the bird taking the mayfly signify a hatch, not only does the flash of color at the break of the riffle signify a fish feeding, but my powers uncoil inside me and I must determine which insect is hatching and what feeding pattern the trout has established. Then I must properly equip myself and properly approach the fish and properly present my imitation. I am engaged in a hunt that is more than a hunt, for the objects of the hunt are mostly to be found within myself, in the nature of my response and action. I am on a Parsifalian quest. I must be scientist, technician, athlete, perhaps even a queer sort of poet.

The Scholar smiles wanly and says, "It all sounds like rank hedonism. And some cultism. With some mumbo jumbo thrown in."

Yes, I am out to pleasure myself, though sometimes after I've been chewed by no-see-ums until I'm pocked like a leper you wouldn't think that. There is a physical testing: the long hours at early morning, in bright sun, or at dusk; casting until your arm is like lead and your legs, from wading against the stiff current, are numb. That is part of the quest: to cleanse through exertion.

And the cultism and mumbo jumbo?

Some of trout fishing has become that, perhaps always was that. It is a separate little world, cunningly contrived, with certain codes and rules and icons. It is not a religion, though some believers make it such, and it is less than an art. But it has qualities of each. It touches heart and head; it demands and builds flexibility and imagination; it is not easy. I come to rivers like an initiate to holy springs. If I cannot draw from them an enduring catechism or from their impulses even very much about "moral evil and of good," they still confer upon me the beneficence of the only deity I have been able to find. And when the little world becomes *too* cunningly contrived? Wit helps.

My friend the Scholar says he is not a puritan or a moralist but that it seems to him it would be more satisfying to make something that would last—a book, a poem, a cabinet, a wooden bowl—than merely to fish well. He quotes Cézanne, from a letter, after a day of fishing: "All this is easier than painting but it does not lead far."

Not hardly. Not very far at all. Except that this may be precisely where I want it to lead. Let the world lead far—as one should frame it to do; let art last long and lead far and to form. Let a few other human activities lead far, though most of them lead us up a tree or up the asshole of the world. Let fly-fishing be temporary and fleeting and inconsequential. I do not mind.

Enough. Enough.

Too much theory and this pleasant respite from the north Broadway renaissance and gray offices will become an extravagant end that leads too far. Fishing is nothing if not a pastime; it would be hell if I did it all the time.

Beyond the dreams and the theories, there are the days when a close friend will pick me up at dawn on my deserted city block and we will make the long drive together, talking, connected, uncoiling, until we reach our river for the day. It is a simple adventure we are undertaking; it is a break from the beetle-dull routine, a new start, an awakening of the senses, a pilgrimage.

Flooded with memories and expectations, we take out our rods, suit up in waders and vest, special fish hats and nets, arrange flies and leaders, and take to the woods. Each article of equipment, each bit of gear in our ritualistic uniform, is part of the act. The skunk cabbage is thrusting up, lush and green-purple out of the moist brown mulch of last year's leaves; we flush a white-tailed deer that bounds off boldly; we

see the pale-green buds pressing out of the birch branches.
"Spring has come again," says Rilke. "The earth is like a
little child who knows poems by heart—many, so many."
We wonder whether the Hendricksons will or will not hatch
at midday. We have our hopes.

With rivers as with good friends, you always feel better for
a few hours in their presence; you always want to review your
dialogue, years later, with a particular pool or riffle or bend,
and to live back through layers of experience. We have been
to this river before and together. We have much to relive.

Then we are on the river. It is still there. So much is per-
ishable, impermanent, dispensable today, so much is gobbled
up by industry and housing and the wanton surge of people,
we half thought it might be gone, like that river we used to
fish in Dutchess County, now bludgeoned by tract homes
and industrial plants and trailers, now littered and warm and
dead. Trout are yardsticks; they are an early warning system
like the canary in the mine—when they go, what will happen
to the rest of the planet, to the quality of life?

Yes, this river is still there, still alive, still pregnant with
possibility.

"There's a swirl," I say, pointing.

"I saw one upstream, too."

"A few flies are coming off, see?"

"Yes, we're going to make a day of it."

My pulse quickens, the long gray city winter vanishes. In a
moment we separate and belong to the river and to its mysteries, to its smooth glides and pinched bends, to the myriad
sweet problems that call forth total concentration, that obvi-
ate philosophy.

Yes, these are Hendricksons, *Ephemerella subvaria*, and
the hatch, on schedule, is just beginning. I am by profession
neither an angler nor a scientist but there's always more
pleasure in knowing than in not knowing. I take the lower

pool and spot four good trout, poised high in the clear, flat water, waiting for the duns to hatch in the riffles and float down. By tilting my head close to the surface, I can see them, like little sailboats, drifting down. Two, three, there's another. Not many yet. A couple of birds are working, dipping and darting; against the light sky above the treeline I pick out one mayfly, watch it flutter, watch a swallow swoop, hesitate, and take it. What looks so pastoral is violent; it is, only on a smaller, more civilized scale, a horde of bluefish slashing a bunker school to bits, leaving blood and fin and head everywhere, to be picked up by the ravenous sea birds. The bites are cleaner here: the birds and trout take a whole creature in one mouthful.

Then back to the river. There are circles below me; the fish are feeding steadily. Shall I fish above or below them? They are so still, so firmly established in an irregular row across the channel in that clear flat water, that I elect the road less traveled and decide to fish down to them on a slack line—this way I won't have to cast over their backs.

It is delicate work, but I know that this year I have an excellent imitation of the natural fly, that my 5X leader is light enough, and that I've done just enough slack-line downstream casting to manage. Fishing is cumulative, though you don't learn all of it, ever.

I position myself carefully on the bank—it would be fatal to wade above such fish—strip about forty feet of line from my reel, and false cast twice.

My rod jerks backward. I've hung my fly in that low brush.

The interruption of the music, like the needle hitting a scratch on a recording of the Brandenburg Concerto, irritates madly but is not final.

When I return, the fish are still feeding, more steadily now, even rhythmically.

My cast lands well above the fish, and my fly floats without drag a few feet short of their feeding station before the line tightens; a little V forms behind the· fly and it goes under.

I retrieve the fly slowly, unwilling to ruffle the surface until there are no more than ten feet of line still in the water, then cast again. The fly floats freely and I hold my breath. This time it will go far enough. It's two feet upstream of the first fish; I'm still holding my breath; the snake in the line unwinds and begins to straighten, slowly, then faster; I lean forward to give it another foot, another few inches; I watch the fish move slightly, turn toward the fly, inspect it, nose up to it, and then the fly drags and the fish turns away.

A deep breath.

Two more casts: one that quarters the river too amply and causes the fly to drag within two feet; another that floats properly but gets there a second after the trout has taken a natural. Then a good cast, a good float, and the fish pivots and takes, feels the hook, jumps twice, and burrows across and upstream. It's thirteen inches and not strong enough to cause much mischief; anyway, after the strike, after I have successfully gulled this creature from another element, linked my brain to its brain, I am less interested. After a few minutes I have the fish near my bank, lean down and twitch the hook free, and it is gone, vigorously—sleek and spotted and still quick.

When I've taken the slime off the fly and air-dried it, I notice that most of the fish have left their stations; only one fish is working in the pool now, across the main current, in a little backwater. It will require a different approach, a different strategy. I take fully five minutes to work my way downstream along the bank, into the water, and across to the other side, moving slowly so as not to disturb the life of the river. I am only its guest. The fish is still working when I get there.

I am directly below the trout now and can see only the periodic circles about forty feet above me. I don't want to put the fly line over it, and I know its actual feeding position in the water will be at least several feet above the mark of the rise form, which is floating downstream and is the final mark of his deliberate inspection ritual. I elect to cast into the edge of the main current above the fish and hope the fly will catch an eddying current and come down into the trout's position. The cast is good. Squinting, I watch the fly float down, then free of, the fast center current and my fly line hug the nearly dead water. There is an electric moment when the circle forms. My arm shoots up. The fish has taken the fly solidly and feels like a good one. It does not jump but bores into its little pool, then into the current; then it gets below me. I slip, recover, and begin to edge downstream, the fish stripping line from the reel now, boiling at the surface twice, then coming upstream quickly while I raise the rod high and haul in line to keep the fish from slipping the hook.

A little later I release the fish from the net, turning it out—a beautiful seventeen-inch brown.

I take two more fish, smaller ones, in the riffle below the pool, then head upstream again to where the first fish were feeding, approaching the spot from below. The hatch has peaked and is tapering now; the late-afternoon chill of late April has set in and I feel it for the first time. One fish is still feeding but I cannot, in six or seven casts, raise it, and finally it stops.

I breathe deeply and take out a pipe. There may be a spinner fall in another hour but I am exhausted. The river is placid, calm now. No fish are rising. The drama is over; the actors have retired to the wings. I have been caught for two hours in an intensely sensual music, and I want to stop, perhaps for the day—to smoke the pipe now, watch that squirrel in the oak, look for deer tracks and chipmunk holes.

The city has become a bad dream, a B movie I once saw that violates my imagination by returning at odd moments. Most of the world would be bored by these past two hours. Most of the world? Most of the world is polluting the rivers, making the worse appear the better cause, peacocking, grating on each other's ears, gouging, putting their fingers on others' souls or their hands in the wrong pockets, scheming, honking, pretending, politicking, small-talking, criticizing.

"Is that *all* you find?" I hear the Scholar ask me.

"Nope. But there's a damned lot of it."

"You're a misanthrope, a hater of cities," he says. "You claim to love gentleness but . . ."

I don't especially want to answer his questions now so I look back at the river. We invented the non sequitur for just such moments.

Yes, we have made a day of it. Two, three hours sandwiched in. Little enough. But deep. And durable. And more than a day's worth. We've earned memories—full and textured—that live now in our very marrowbones, that make us more alive. Our thoughts will be greener, our judgments perhaps sharper, our eyes a bit brighter. We live day to day with little change in our perceptions, but I never go to a river that I do not see newly and freshly, that I do not learn, that I do not find a story.

On the way home I still feel the tug of the river against my thighs, and in my mind's eye I can see that largest rising trout, the neat circle when it took a natural, the quick dramatic spurt—electric through my whole body—when it took my fly and I felt its force. And I wondered why I had not raised that last fish.

It was not the ultimate river, the ultimate afternoon; it was not so exquisite as a Keatsian moment frozen and anguished because it would not last. There will be others—never equal,

always discretely, sharply different. A thousand such moments. Days when, against all expectation, the river is dead;
days when it is generous beyond dreams.

A luxury? A mere vacation?

No, those rivers are more. They are my Pilgrim Creek and
Walden Pond, however briefly. Those rivers and their
bounty—bright and wild—touch me and through me touch
every person whom I meet. They are a metaphor for life. In
their movement, in their varied glides, runs, and pools, in
their inevitable progress toward the sea, they contain many of
the secrets we seek to understand about ourselves, our purposes. The late Roderick Haig-Brown said, "Were it not for
the strong, quick life of rivers, for their sparkle in the sun-
shine, for the cold grayness of them under rain and the feel
of them about my legs as I set my feet hard down on rocks or
sand or gravel, I should fish less often." Amen. When such
rivers die, as so many have, so too dies an irretrievable part of
the soul of each of the thousands of anglers who in their
waters find deep, enduring life.

Visit a few of them with me. We won't linger long. I know
how fearfully busy and hurried you are. But perhaps a few
moments will be of some profit. Perhaps you will meet some
old friends, smile (without seeking to gull someone thereby),
and make a new friend or two as we travel: first near, then
far.

Part One

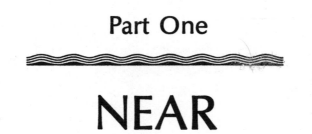

NEAR

1
Pilgrimages

And smale fowles maken melodye,
That slepen al the night with open yë,
(So priketh hem nature in hir corages):
Than longen folk to goon on pilgrimages.
GEOFFREY CHAUCER

I was not born near rivers and I have not lived my life near
them. From the beginning, my fishing has been a matter of
excursions. Usually I went for a day, perhaps two days at a
fling. For this I would prepare weeks, sometimes months in
advance, buying new bits of tackle to meet new knowledge
I'd acquired, tying leaders, rewinding guides, selecting the
proper flies, lures, or, much earlier, bait.

In my teens these were massive, exhausting treks, beginning in dark basements in Brooklyn at three in the morning,
ending when I returned at midnight. Everything was carried
in great packs on my back—waders, gear, extra clothing,
food, all. Had not some friends got the use of the family car
when we were seventeen, I would to this day be hump-
backed.

That first day out in April was—and is—holy to me. It
always meant the first break of the year with the gray, indoor
winter. I need it to freshen my eye, to remind me that I can

27

still explore, adventure. It is a beginning and augurs a wealth of days from then until autumn, when the bright rivers will be available, waiting. My feet pick up a quicker pace those first few days in April; my wife says my eyes light up. In my green years I did not miss an Opening Day—but now the season begins somewhat later, under less frenzied, less crowded conditions. I have learned to wait. Another week, another few days will not matter that much. Not now. I could still bear that cold, with the ice freezing at the guides, and no doubt some fish can be taken on a fly. Some fly-fishermen I know even make a ritual of the day, complete with a traditional lunch or breakfast at home or at a favorite restaurant; some seek chiefly the celebration—more natural than a Lincoln's or Washington's birthday—of the new year. Who can blame them?

Chaucer begins his *Canterbury Tales* with such a magnificent celebration of the power of spring. When April with its sweet showers pierces to the root "the droghte of Marche," and small birds, too filled, apparently, with the excitement of spring to close their eyes, sing all night, then "longen folk to goon on pilgrimages. . . ."

It is a pilgrimage indeed. Chaucer's "palmers" come from various parts of England and travel to Canterbury, to seek the "holy blisful martir," who has helped them "whan that they were seke. . . ." Fly-fishermen, with little less zeal, seek moving water again. They want to touch that which is awake, alive. All is awake. All begins again. Sometimes, deep in the city, the first touch of spring, a wraithlike dream—green and bright and flowing—seeps through the gray and starts the awakening. Or perhaps, on dark forsythia branches still flecked with snow, bright green buds appear.

All is growing. *Anthony* has grown. I measure him with my eye and see that he is older, calmer, less a child, more a bud about to bloom. Perhaps he is old enough this year. Perhaps. Certainly he's willing. All that winter he had been after me: "Dad. Dad. You promised. Can I go with you and Mike? Can I?"

His older brothers always got the largest piece of cake; he always wore their hand-me-downs; he always got interrupted at the table. But he is older now, pushing thirteen, holding his own, full of his own mischief and play and purpose. I have tried, with mixed success, to convert people I love to this fly-fishing I love; I do so no more. It is, after all, a private affair and must come or not come as it will. But since I talk fishing *ad nauseam* and find few listeners any more in my own home, I leap upon Anthony's interest. The addict needs allies.

What is this hook?

Sparse Grey Hackle says that "you will search far to find a fisherman to admit that a taste for fishing, like a taste for liquor, must be governed lest it come to possess its possessor." I cringe when I think of those times when my taste for it has come to possess me: the long hours snatched from employment that would lead further, when I've tinkered with tackle, tied flies, eyed choice bamboo rods at Abercrombie's (which I could scarcely afford), gabbed incessantly with other addicts, thought fish, read fish, dreamed fish. For while the worries vanished, so did my commitments. I'd return three hours late, my ears filled with the rush of the river, frizzled, freaked out on fly hatches, my wife livid, her gold wedding band gleaming brightly on the top of my Tackle Satchel. Once, when Sunday driving with my family, watching the river more than the road, as I always do, hearing my wife say, as she always does when I'm driving near water, "You're on the shoulder again, Nick," I spotted the telltale spreading-circle rise of a good trout. There was nothing to be done. I

screeched to a stop and, mumbling to my wife and four impatient young children to be patient (the classic fisherman's,
if not fisherman's family's, virtue), set up my everhandy rod
and galloped like a bison straight for the stream. My wife
claims that she reminded me I had on new shoes and new
slacks, that she advised me, with her good prudence, at least
to put on waders. I don't remember. Later, we scarcely said
two civil words to each other for three hours. No doubt
because I'd ruined my shoes. I tried to tell her why I'd lost
the trout but she wouldn't listen, she wouldn't hear another
word about "the contemplative man's recreation."

I cannot give up a rising trout any more than I can the
search for the irresistible fly, the ultimate fly rod. I am forever searching for a better leader formula, a more efficient
vest, an answer to this or that trout mystery. Why wasn't
there a rise at two o'clock on the Green House Pool? There
was one last year at that time. Why did the Lady Blitz work
well at dusk last night, not tonight? Why, when trout were
rising all afternoon, couldn't I even raise a chub?

Why?

That, I suspect, is the ultimate hook. Men by nature desire
to know; trout by nature are capricious, mysterious, unpre-
dictable—at least to me. Your disposition, their disposition,
maybe even the phase of the moon affects the outcome.
Nothing is certain in trout fishing, says Arnold Gingrich,
"except its glorious uncertainty."

Of course there are days when, miraculously, all goes
well—when you are far from the quiet desperations, closer to
nature than you've ever been, calm and contemplative, when
the flies hatch on schedule and you have the right fly and the
fish become particularly human in their predictability. I've
had a few such days when nearly every cast brought a trout.

"And you weren't bored?" the Scholar asks.

No.

"And that didn't satisfy your longing to strike through the 'pasteboard mask' veiling the elusive mystery?"

No. No more than catching nothing bores the addicted angler. Catching fish and not catching fish are both drugs. Each hungers where most it satisfies.

"But you can't always fish," says the father of Roland Pertwee's boy-addict in *The River God*.

"I told him I could, and I was right and have proved it for thirty years and more."

"Well, well," the father, like any good condescending nonangler, says, "please yourself, but isn't it dull not catching anything?"

And the boy answers, as he does a thousand times thereafter (even as I have done a thousand times), "As if it could be."

Would Anthony be bored? Did he know how cold it would be in April? "That doesn't bother me, Dad. You know." Did he realize, his mother advised, that old Dad *talked* good fly-fishing but—so it seemed—rarely caught anything? "I'll catch some for him." Did he *really* know, one of his brothers asked, how downright boring it could be? "Dad doesn't get bored." Nope. Not ever. Not for one minute of it.

Well, we would try.

We picked Mike Migel up at eight on a cold gray mid-April morning. Anthony knew and liked him. What twelve-year-old wouldn't like that tall thin white-haired gentleman, with a handshake that gobbles up your fingers with a firm warmth. And he tells stories, too! Wide-eyed and unusually silent, the boy listened as Mike began to tell about growing up in Arizona a half century ago. We began, at the George Washington Bridge, with the Apache massacre in which one of Mike's uncles died, before Mike went to live on the ranch, and progressed quickly to the sheep dog that used to lie beneath the porch on a hot day and nip a bit of the tail off the pet monkey whenever he could; he'd gotten all but a couple of inches of it, during the course of a summer, when we shifted abruptly to the lion hunt. The lion hunt! No sooner were the words out than the boy's eyes widened like a camera lens, catching everything. Mike was only fourteen and went with some men down into Mexico where a lion had been lunching on some unfortunate townspeople. They took guns and mules and tracking dogs. I glanced from the road to the boy's face. The story continued ever so slowly with substories about Mike's first use of a gun, about tracking other wild and dangerous beasts, and we had just picked up the sure scent of this particular cat when we discovered we were two hours upstate already and that it was time for coffee before hitting the river. We hoped the Hendricksons would be hatching. But we were early—they wouldn't be off for another few hours.

In the diner Anthony kept looking at Mike and finally asked, "Well, what happened? Did you get the lion?"

"There's a remarkable story concerning that."

The boy waited.

Mike finished his bite of a doughnut.

"It'll take some time," Mike said. "Perhaps we should save it for the trip back, Anthony."

"Well . . . I'd just as soon hear it now. If that's okay."

I said, "We've got to plan out the fishing now."

"Oh. Does it have to be planned?"

Perhaps not. But that adds to the pleasure. So we talked leaders and flies and particularly choice days in the bright past and, after some debate, chose our section of the river for the day, and after a half hour I could tell that Anthony rightly considered all this trout talk somewhat less important than lions.

Or maybe he didn't.

An hour or so later, Mike and I were a hundred yards apart in a cold, deep riffle below the Big Bend. It was far colder than we'd thought, the water in the high thirties, the air not much warmer. There was still no sun. It had begun to drizzle steadily. At the bend, a long flat glide turned with deceptive speed into a treacherous, sweeping rapids. I was fishing a Red Quill upstream, a bit too quickly, without great expectations; Mike, from a fixed position below the bend, where the pinched flow began to widen, was fishing a wet fly in the currents, casting slightly upstream, mending, letting the fly work as slowly and deeply as possible. We'd been at it for an hour and the signs were not good. The water was too heavy and too cold; no flies had shown—and wouldn't; we were too early for this run to produce. We shouldn't have chosen a river so far north.

But it was the first day out and I could feel a deep stillness inside me. I enjoyed casting; I enjoyed watching Mike cast. But we were too early, much too early; the green was still sleeping in the alders and the trout were slow.

While I worked rapidly upstream toward Mike, I could see Anthony fishing along the bank above us. His white face glistened out of the dark low alder branches and surrounding grasses.

"Anything at all?" I asked Mike.

"A tap. Maybe two."

"Any size?"

"Couldn't tell."

"I don't think any flies will show."

"I saw two. Exactly two. Quill Gordons, I suppose."

"It's a start. We're a week early. By Thursday, if it warms, they should . . . Anthony!"

The boy had waded out into the glide in his brother's

baggy chest waders. He was coming toward us. "Anthony! Go around! The water's too deep there. Too fast. Don't try to wade! Go through!"

Had he heard me?

The sound of the bend rapids was a steady rush in my ears.

Mike started to move brusquely upstream. I followed, rushing now against the heavy press of the current. I knew that stretch. The boy was not going to make it. I waved him back frantically. I shouted. Didn't he hear me? Mike kept moving quickly around the curved edge of the bend.

Then, while we were still fifty yards from him, hopelessly too far, I froze, then lunged forward again, up to Mike, past him. Anthony started to lose his balance as the current quickened. We could tell his feet had slipped; we could see his small body twist and struggle against the greater force of the water. He slid forward now, almost racing at us, weirdly, as the water leaped toward the turn. Then he was off his feet and under, all the way under, over his head, splashing, flailing out, his feet out from under him now, then up, fear in his eyes for the first time, his movements jerky, wild, as the water deepened and sped out toward the fastest white-capped broken water where we'd never be able to reach him.

"Anthony! No! No!"

But then he was up somehow, with a toehold, and we breathed deeply as he lunged toward the bank, *willing* himself there—slipping back, forcing himself on, safe.

In a small covert among high dead grasses, in the cold wet air, we stripped off his jacket, slacks, shirt, undershirt, underpants, socks, everything. He stood stark still and wide eyed, unashamed, shaking only slightly, as we wrung out each bit of clothing: silent, white, like something sprung suddenly from winter earth on a spring afternoon.

An hour later I was still shaking.

It had been as close as it can get.

In the warm car, heading home, with my old fishing coat snug around him, Anthony sat like a prince. Mike and I talked about the two flies he had seen, the one I saw later and positively identified as a Quill Gordon, and then Anthony heard all about the lion, in effusive detail, and he said, "You guys don't catch anything but you sure have fun out here."

He and I fished together on brisk, misty mornings in May; and then in June, standing by my side in the Esopus River, he caught his first trout on a fly. And last week, as the time for another pilgrimage approached, he came over to my desk one night, hung on my shoulder, and said, "About this book you're writing, Dad. I mean, you'd better get it done in time, by April, so we guys don't lose any of our fly-fishing time."

A month after Anthony's first trip, I took another pilgrimage with Mike, to the big Delaware. I'd never fished it before.

Mike was an hour late, which was all right because he's often late and the fishing didn't start, he'd told me, until "very late in the day." Then he was two hours late, and it was ten o'clock, and by the time he finally showed—his dark-blue Pontiac rounding the corner of my city block—I would have given up on the trip and gone back to bed had my expectations not been so high.

We were going to fish for rainbows with Ed Van Put, and I had been looking forward to the trip for weeks.

The lateness was simply explained. Mike had left his car in front of his apartment building for a few minutes while he went back for a second fly rod he'd leaned against the elevator. When he returned, the car was being lifted behind a police tow truck. He shouted, they were deaf; he pleaded, they drove off. He had to follow the truck by cab to the city lot and pay a $75 fine to retrieve it. One never extricates one-self from the city easily. It must love us too well.

Well, there was a long, rich day ahead of us, and those "muscular rainbows" Mike had described danced in my imagination. I speculated as we drove that for the overworked inner-city angler, fishing often became less *what* than *who* you knew. I was going to be admitted to Kafka's Castle with-out delay that afternoon. No more for me the long disastrous escapes from the city—driving hundreds of miles to barren streams, meeting crowds or high water, fishing an hour too late or leaving an hour too early, arriving a day after con-struction started upriver and the water was in cocoa-colored spate; no more the exhaustion and frustration and discovery, three hours from the city, that what I'd labored so hard to get to was not there.

Now, instead of trips randomly stolen from the maelstrom of the city, I more and more made the long up-country pil-grimage when I had good information. "Hi, Nick, my boy," would come Art Flick's hearty voice on the phone. "They started coming off today. You ought to get up within the next few days while they're still strong. The 'Kill, eight miles below the bridge, above Old Oak Pool. I'll be there tomorrow at noon if you want to meet me." An offer too good to refuse. With that kind of advice one foregoes the sage advice that the best time to fish is when you can. The best time to fish is when Art Flick tells you to fish. As I proved next day. The Hendricksons began to hatch and the fish to rise, right on schedule, and I was actually there, at the right place and right time, with the guy who wrote the book and who had given me some of his Red Quills, which imitate the male of the species, as all initiates know. Who couldn't have caught fish? Even *I* got a few.

This remarkable principle worked for me in Provincetown,

thanks to the "swami of the surf," Frank Woolner, and on the Yellowstone River, thanks to Charlie Brooks. Clearly I had the system beat, the inscrutable mysteries of trout fishing solved. Or thought I did—forgetting that time and chance and the fickleness of fish and my own brand of city-bred ineptitude happeneth to me quite often.

A well-planned and advised trip to Henrys Lake, that extraordinary fishery in Idaho, ended in near-disaster when I managed, with much effort, to get my fly line caught in the Johnson 15-horsepower motor. That's not easy to do. I tipped the motor up to get in at the blades and began to pick away the weed and untangle the line. When the motor kept slipping down, I leaned farther out, to get beneath it. I'd taken out six or seven healthy clumps of weed and unwrapped the line a couple of turns, when the motor slipped again and I with it. I lost control, dunked my head in upside down up to my nose, rammed my leg against the gunwale so hard I could barely walk for a week, jerked myself back up and into the boat, kicked the plug out so water began rushing into the bottom like a reservoir sluice, rubbed my head, wiped the water out of my eyes, cursed my leg, shoved the plug back in, and tipped the boat so violently I almost fell into the lake again.

Even expert advice cannot keep you from a trick like that. It takes practice.

For years I'd heard rumors about the increasingly good fishing for large rainbows in the Delaware River, and the name Ed Van Put came up repeatedly. As a Catskill-region fish-and-wildlife technician, he was both a knowledgeable biologist and a man with regular access to and understanding of the river. Mike had met him, and we were going to be taken by Ed to one of the best pools on the Delaware. I couldn't miss.

There were a few chores first: to visit a house Mike might

want to rent, then over to Len Wright's cabin on the Neversink, to pick him up. By the time we finally met Ed at four
o'clock at the Roscoe Diner, I was exhausted; it had been
eight hours since I'd officially started on this fishing trip, and
though the company was good I was anxious to be on the
water—this was beginning to look too much like all those
bumbling trips I'd made before I got authoritative advice.

Besides, it had started to rain—first steadily, then fiercely,
then not at all, then steadily again. There was a time when I
didn't much mind fishing in the rain in early summer, in
fact thought it brought better fishing, but I was older now
and didn't have a rain jacket with me; about six years earlier
when I'd gone outside my apartment to wait for Mike, it had
been sunny.

We packed into two cars, and Mike followed Ed upstate,
along Route 17, to the Delaware. It would have been downright unsociable and cowardly of me to ask, but I rather wondered what the bar of the Antrim Lodge looked like at this
time of day. An hour later, about five o'clock, we headed
down a dead-end muddy road, stopped, stretched, suited up,
and headed for the river.

It was still raining—not as hard but steadily. I tried to light
my cigar but it kept fizzling out.

What a river! Its huge sweeping turns were more than a
half mile long; where we came out of the woods, there was
nothing to indicate the hand of man but an old railroad
track. Clusters of aspen, willow, birch, and alder graced the
far side of the river. Some rhododendron was in bloom. This
was a gloriously wild stretch, equal to anything I'd seen out
west, and only—at least that day—nine hours from the city.
As my eye swept down the length of the river, I saw fish
breaking water only a few hundred yards away. They were
obviously big fish, in the shallows, and there were a lot of

them. Good grief, I'd fish in a hailstorm for creatures like that! They were monsters. I'd hit a bonanza again and was all for trotting down the tracks in my waders to get at them.

"Shad," said Ed. "Probably spent, and almost impossible to catch. They'll be heading downstream in another week or so."

We marched slowly down the tracks in the rain, watching the water constantly. This was as lovely a stretch of river as I could remember ever having seen. Ed said it would be lovelier if the reservoir people let a steady flow of cold water out from the bottoms of Cannonsville and the Pepacton. He said that in another few weeks the water would become so warm that fishing would stop and the fish might die. It sounded criminal.

"What's the drill?" Len asked when we got to the bend Ed wanted to fish. We'd walked about a mile in the rain.

An Adams or Gray Fox Variant, about size 16, would be best; we might pick up a fish or two during the next hour or so, but the real fishing would start at dusk. Ed did better than catch a fish or two. In ten minutes he was into a really large rainbow that took him into his backing. Then he had another on, then another. He'd earlier told me he'd caught more than two hundred rainbows each of the past two years, most of them over fifteen inches and at least forty or fifty over eighteen. Today, no one else caught even a chub. For me that was not surprising, but I'd expected more of Len and Mike.

I fished from the tail of the sweeping pool up into the run where the current struggled to keep its definition, then into the fast, choppy water, then into the head of the riffle— thinking that the rainbows might go into the fastest water during the day. The trouble was, besides not seeing a fish— except the ones on Ed's line—I couldn't keep a cigar lit; ei-

ther I'd get one started only to have the rain snuff it out a
moment later or I'd spend ten minutes trying fruitlessly to
light a soggy cigar with damp matches. I fish better with a lit
cigar; some people fish better with talent. But I fished downstream diligently with a large Whitlock Bronze Nymph,
which had raised some good fish for me in the West, and
watched Ed catch still another muscular rainbow. He casts
an immaculately slow and graceful line, and I had the dis-
tinct impression that he was also doing something I didn't
see, like humming or whistling to these old finny friends to
perform for the crowd. He could tell by his taggings that he'd
caught several of these fish before; no doubt they were aware
that he released every fish he caught and thus had no reluc-
tance to renew acquaintance.

As for me, I sloshed around despondently, bone tired now,
whipping the water to a froth, getting wetter by the minute,
wondering precisely why I wasn't home reading *The Turn of
the Screw* instead of making such a fool of myself. This was
strictly a regression.

But finally, about eight forty, just after the light grew dim,
two splendid events took place: the rain stopped and the fish
began to rise ferociously, dozens of them. I promptly lit a
new cigar, clipped off my large nymph, and rummaged in
one of my fly boxes for a No. 16 Adams. Well, I was going to
make a day of it at last—or at least a fifteen minutes of it. I
could *taste* the rise and run of one of those sleek rainbows.

My hands began to tremble. All the old fever and expectation returned, all fatigue vanished. I fumbled with the fly,
couldn't get the leader point through the eye of the hook,
raised the fly against the dun sky, manipulated the thin monofilament with the deftness of a surgeon, and at last got the
pesky thing done.

Eight forty-five, and nearly dark.

The circles—rhythmic and gentle—continued to spread in the flat water where the current widened. Ed was at my left shoulder now, willing to forego these fine last moments of the day so he could advise me. A saint.

"Cast to specific rises, Nick, as delicately as possible. Some of these are really big fish. Over twenty inches. Strike them lightly."

With not a second to lose, I took my dry-fly spray from my vest, held the Adams near my face, pressed the plunger—and went stingingly blind. The little hole had been pointed in the wrong direction. I'd given myself a triple shot of fly dope in the eyes, and even after I doused them with a bit of the Delaware I could barely see.

But I squinted bravely, puffed with vigor on my cigar—whose tip now glowed like a hot little coal in the dark—and began to cast in the general direction Ed was pointing.

"That looked about right," he said as I laid out a surprisingly accurate cast to one of the inviting circles. I couldn't see the fly but that didn't matter.

"Can't imagine why he didn't take it," Ed said.

When I miraculously repeated the feat, a good cast, he said, "They're awfully picky sometimes. What have you got on?"

"A sixteen Adams."

"That *ought* to do it."

Another cast, my third good one in a row, a record. It was a magical, witching moment, the far bank receding in the swirling mists, the river sounds filling my ears, my squinting eyes seeing only that faint multitude of spreading circles. I could not see my fly but knew exactly where it was by estimating the distance from the end of my bright yellow fly line.

Nothing.

"Strange," said Ed.

"Maybe this time."

Still nothing—and nothing for the next fifteen minutes, when a moonless sky finally pulled the curtain on us and we began to head back up the long stretch of railroad tracks to the cars.

In the headlights I saw a strange sight, which I took the liberty of not reporting to my fellow anglers. There was no fly on my leader! There was only a blackened, melted end, as if, just possibly, it might have been burned through by a cigar.

Mike and I made the long trip back in silence. Had I really fished through the entire rise, the twenty minutes I'd waited for all day, with no fly? No doubt. I was capable of it. My face still smarted in the darkened car with embarrassment, my eyes still stung. I tried to keep my eyelids from drooping, and I tried to talk—because good talk with a good friend after a long day on a river is one of the best parts of any trip. But I was bushed.

I closed my eyes and dreamed of muscular rainbows dimpling to a No. 16 Adams, then skyrocketing out and taking me into the backing. That huge bend of the river was alive with rising fish and each cast was true. I heard Ed say, "They're awfully picky sometimes. What have you got on?"

And I answered, moaning, knowing I had developed a pattern even the experts had never thought of, "The emperor's new fly!"

2
Experts and Friends

Whatsoever thy hand findeth to do, do it with thy might; for there is no work, nor device, nor knowledge, nor wisdom, in the grave, whither thou goest.

ECCLESIASTES

THERE are advantages to being known as a fly-fishing expert. People send you free flies and ask for your opinion of the thorax tie; you get to try out (and keep) marvelous new equipment and to take paid trips to storied rivers where brown trout grow as long as one of Wilt's stilts; other fly-fishermen make a happy fuss over your mere presence; you can become a well-paid consultant, a lecturer on the trout-talk beat, an author, a panelist, a clinic instructor. Being an expert massages the wallet and the ego. Some people even make a living at it.

I always wanted to be an expert. It seemed a good kind of creature to be. I especially dreamed of being asked to fish the bright rivers of Argentina, New Zealand, Iceland, Wales. Being an expert would without fail put me in dramatic connection with rivers. But though it grieves me to do so, I am forced to confess that I am not—and never will be—an expert. Not only am I an amateur but I am about to become an

43

apologist for amateurs. Amateur fly-fishers, that is. For if a man is going to write or act or sing or paint or fix plumbing or carburetors for his supper—or his soul—he should try to be the best he can be at it, the best there is. "Whatsoever thy hand findeth to do, do it with thy might," sayeth the preacher, and he is no doubt right.

But *not* about fly-fishing?

Well, we do it chiefly for recreation, don't we? It is, in the best sense of the word, a pastime, isn't it? Most of us fly-fish for the sheer pleasure of it, to heal the sores of work—to refresh, pursue, make whole again. At least that's what I thought until I started trying too hard to become an expert. *That* nearly killed my love of rivers.

Frankly, the problem became this: near and far, as far as two thousand miles from home, friends and perfect strangers—out of a variety of false assumptions (mistaking passion for expertise, labeling me by association with my betters)—actually considered me to be an expert. Alas. There is a time in every man's life when he must see himself for what he is. It is not so. It will never be so. My grasp of Latin entomological names is rotten and improves not at all; I spend too little time on the rivers I love; I am mostly inept, careless; I mismatch the hatch and slap the back cast; despite my most patient patching, even my waders leak.

Witness this bogus expert during a splendid caddis hatch on a popular section of the Yellowstone River in the park. The little gray whirlers are coming off in clouds. Cutthroats—fifteen, sixteen, seventeen inches—are lying high in the water, tipping their pretty snouts up to take the duns. Everywhere you look trout are rising in the clear, riffled flow. Charlie Brooks has brought me. He has seen this before; I have not. My blood, which should be cool, turns to a swift boil. Did I actually froth at the mouth? Maybe. It would have been consonant with my mood. I rummage around in my vest and pluck out the only reel I've brought, forgetting until that moment that I'd lent the reel to one of my sons, who'd gotten such a brilliantly complex series of wind knots in the leader that I'd cut it through a foot below the nail knot.

My hands tremble. I look out at the Yellowstone and those cutthroats have gone berserk. There must be a thousand of them. Charlie, who has indeed seen this before, says, "Problem with your leader? Let me tie a new one to that stub." He has (may his leaders never rot!) a special knot for tying thinner diameter monofilament to twenty-five-pound-test butts. Who'd have thought the problem would ever come up? Who'd have thought that an expert like me would be ignorant enough to come to the river without an adequate leader? Actually, I had been on the verge of trying to push that fat stub through the eye of one of George Bodmer's deadly Colorado Kings, size 16.

I have come as Charlie's editor, and though I have made no boasts I fear he now thinks me the perfect fool.

Well, he gets the thing done, patiently instructing me as he does, though I hear none of it since I'm looking mostly at the river, and I string up the rod, turn and head for the river, turn again to thank him, trip and nearly bust my rod, and arrive at what must be the closest thing to heaven—a river alive with rising trout.

Two casts from the bank and I've got something: a seventy-foot pine tree. Unlike most of the large things I hook, it does not shake free, nor can I disengage it before Charlie comes over and politely plucks it out for me. The third cast stays cunningly out of the trees—and hooks me neatly in the earlobe. I have fished for more than thirty-five years and have only heard of this embarrassing phenomenon. Play it non-

chalant, Nick, I think, and say, "Got a clipper, Charlie? I
just want to snip this barb. . . ."

The man still hasn't rigged his rod—is he human?—so he
comes over, looks at the sweet little thing in my ear, and
says, "Out here we just pull them straight back out."

"Real-ly?"

"Sure. Only stings for a moment."

"That's the way they do it out here, is it? Straight
back . . ."

And the thing is out.

Though these huge cutthroats are rising no more than a
foot from shore, in the little eddies beside our bank, in the
first riffles, I decide to wade out. Perhaps it's safer out there.
But the current is stronger than it looks, and naturally I have
not replaced my worn felts this year; soon I am safely stuck
between two rocks, there for the afternoon or longer, and
flailing away. When I manage to snag a few of these generous fish and see that Charlie has caught a few and put down
his rod, I feel much more relaxed. He's a friend, after all, not
a judge. But turning toward the bank after releasing a fish, I
notice that Charlie is now talking to several fishermen. They
begin to watch me intently—and promptly everything goes
wrong again. My line tangles in my net; I try to take a step
and nearly keel over in the current. Then I try an especially
long cast and the line does not come forward after the back
cast. I have hooked another cutthroat—on the slap as it
were—and try desperately to pretend I had fished it that way.
Do they know? Do they see the blood on my ear? Does one
of them have a camera?

I am an expert at hindsight. Ten minutes after I've left a
luncheon at which I babbled and mumbled, failed miserably
at comebacks and bons mots, I become extraordinarily brilliant. Walking home, I become like one of the other maniacs

on upper Broadway, laughing and giggling out loud to the tune of some hidden inner dialogue; my wit and courage astound me. Some people's minds work like that: ten minutes too late at a minimum. Mine does. Always.

I'm also not bad at second-guessing my fishing mistakes. In the late fall or in the dead of winter, when I've put all my rods and tackle in order and safely away, I can think of a dozen things I should have done had I been even part expert.

Many of these things fall into the category of tackle care, a subject I flunk regularly. The slightest piece of equipment reminds me: leaky waders, a broken leader clipper, sunglasses that should have been Polaroid. A quick look in my fish closet and I know why my casts hooked and fell awkwardly on that last trip: my fly line has a bad crack above the nail knot. Had I been *that* unconscious on the stream? Why hadn't I noticed it? And even if I had, would I have had the skill and patience to clip the raw end and tie on a new leader with a good nail knot? Not hardly.

And why hadn't I rewound the frayed winding on a middle guide of my fly rod instead of having to pull a Band-Aid off my scratched finger to keep the guide in place? It would have taken me no more than ten minutes to do at home, and I knew it had to be done.

While I am asking myself such embarrassing questions, I notice the fly box still in my vest, which reminds me that— with twenty good grasshopper imitations in my storage case—I took only mayfly patterns with me in early September. The fields had been full of plump, leaping grasshoppers, and I got skunked on mayfly imitations. Was I saving those Whitlock Hoppers for Opening Day?

Hindsight? I'm flush with it.

So much for would-be experts who had once the longing but never the hand. What about the real thing?

There's Flick, of course, who's more than an expert: he's a fisherman. He's so skillful that I had to fish with him a handful of times before I realized he was not a magician. He'd caught a half dozen good trout in the middle of a hot July afternoon on the Battenkill—when *no one* catches trout—and another half dozen one evening on the Schoharie when I didn't see a fish move; before a Hendrickson hatch one early May afternoon, he'd taken a fat eighteen-inch brown from high roiled water when I'd had trouble casting, knowing where to fish, or what fly to use.

But I finally realized that he wasn't a magician, a trout hypnotist, a possessor of occult wisdom. Nothing of the sort. He doesn't even think like a trout. He's merely an enormously skillful and practical fly-fisherman who has reduced the great mysteries of the sport to a minimal number of working and effective maxims—and, while others fret and puzzle over complexities, debate esoteric theories, and fiddle with their fine bamboo and nine thousand flies, he has fun.

And he catches fish.

Of course Art has one great advantage over most of us. Though he isn't a professional fish expert—one of that peripatetic breed who roam the world over—he can fish virtually every day of the open season, and this is exactly what he has done for the past forty or fifty years, fishing every inch of the fifteen or sixteen miles of his beloved Schoharie. For years he fished no other river, but he missed little. The Schoharie is blessed with every important kind of water: turbulent runs, bright riffles, pocket water, pools.

The Flick magic is simplicity. He once spotted a man on the Schoharie, taking literally dozens of fly boxes out of his pockets and putting them on a rock. He thought the man must have fallen in, was drying out his flies, and rushed to his aid.

"Can I help?" he called.

The man looked up, scowled, and said, "You can if you've got a computer. I've got so many darn fly patterns I can't keep track of them."

Art has insisted for years that "less is more" is a better maxim for the trout fisherman to live—and fish—by than "more is better." His *Streamside Guide* stresses just this, and he himself uses remarkably few patterns. He uses his own simple, spare dressings for the principal Catskill hatches: the Quill Gordon, the Hendrickson, the March Brown, the Cahill, the Gray Fox, and several others, but when there are no flies hatching he invariably fishes his favorite Gray Fox Variant (the best all-purpose fly I've ever used) or, recently, his Dun Variant in the later season. His basic equipment is as simple as the fly patterns he carries. Though he once, at Ray Bergman's urging, sold Dickerson bamboo fly rods (they sold for $60 then, are collector's items at nearly $400 now), Art prefers a balanced Scientific Anglers glass rod, No. 4 for most dry-fly work, No. 5 when it's necessary to go a bit heavier. ("Any man who would spend $300 for a fly rod, which can be broken in some fluke accident," he says, "ought to have his head examined.") He uses a twelve-foot leader early in the season and increases this to thirteen or fourteen feet as the water drops and grows clearer. His vest is sparsely furnished with a few flies appropriate for the day, a privately made clip-on container for fly dope, a good knife, and an ancient tear-drop net. His approach is always simple, functional. He's even modest enough to say of his methods, "For someone who has fished as long and as hard as I have, I am probably the worst fly-fisherman in the world. I pay little attention to technique, use only the two or three basic casts. All those fancy, complicated casts! They're taking the fun out of fishing." His casts are merely straight, quick, and true. They merely send the fly where the trout is. They merely get the fly onto the water more than it's in the air. That's all.

So. Part of the mystery of Flick is this: He fishes one river and knows it better than any man alive (and can translate his knowledge of the Schoharie's pools and runs to his infrequent forays to Montana, where he caught a 5½-pound brown in the Yellowstone several years ago, to Labrador, and to several other Catskill rivers); he knows fly-fishing from its roots, the water he's worked at preserving, the trout-stream insects he's collected, charted, and written about; he has been a guide and fished day after day through more than fifty seasons; and he has unflinching confidence in a few of his own proven fly patterns. He goes out at the right times, keeps his fly on the water, and catches fish. He's a fisherman first, an expert merely by virtue of his excellence at it.

"For the average person," Art says, "every time you add complications, new gadgets, more flies, the chances of taking fish go down. There's simply less time left for the fishing itself."

Art moves faster and has his fly on the water far more than any other man I've seen or heard of; frankly, I'd say he fishes five times as fast as the average fisherman, even at seventy-two. "If your fly isn't on the water," he says with a light laugh, "you can't catch any fish." He also knows his river so well that he's always thinking of the spot "just a little upstream" where he raised a good trout the year before, and he will know more quickly than most that there are no fish in a particular spot that he can catch. For pocket-water fishing, which he insists is too often overlooked by fly-fishermen but which he likes best, you *have* to fish fast. "Anyway, I'd go crazy," he says, "to go to one pool and stay there, like so many fishermen do, for a long period of time. That's one reason I don't like pool fishing, except the last thing in the day. It's not in my nature."

Fitting his nature to his fishing, Art has become incredibly adept at pocket-water and riffle fishing. Those half dozen trout he took from the Battenkill at midday were from the riffles, where the trout have more cover during the day, more oxygen—and are cooler. "Fishing the riffles," he says, "you must be alert every second. More often than not you won't even see the fly taken, just the hit. You have to concentrate every minute and forget everything else."

From his knowledge of water, weather, and entomology, Art has a sure sense of when fish will be available for the taking. You do not appear on a stream at four in the morning to fish a Hendrickson hatch that will appear in the early afternoon; at best, you come a few hours early to fish the nymphs that will be active then. He is also, today, less interested in the less selective, smaller fish—a natural evolution—and fishes when there is a decent chance of taking a tough, larger trout. There is another reason Art spends less time on the water today. It's not his age; I'm nearly thirty years his junior and he'll wear me out any day.

"Lots of times now," he told me confidentially, "when March Browns or Gray Foxes are on the water, I'll be on the stream in the late morning or afternoon, when they should be coming. But if they don't I think of my long-suffering wife"—so he has one, too!—"who has never said one word about my fishing, or when I should or shouldn't fish, in fifty years." Mine has. "I just haven't got the heart to stay out on the stream anymore, and lots of times now the flies will come after I've gone home to dinner. Back in the old days, I'd want to be there. I wouldn't miss one minute of it. But I've gotten over that feeling." He pauses reflectively, then adds, "If I don't catch them today, I'll catch them another day."

Art Flick, fisherman, usually does.

There's also another breed of expert. A friend of mine once spotted one of these bona-fide famous people far downriver on some choice club water in the East. From coast to coast the bards sang of this man's exploits in the white wine-tinted glides. So my friend relinquished a perfectly good night of fishing and, like a sleuth or secret agent, crept into the bushes and took up his surveillance. It might prove more valuable than any book he'd ever read to watch this expert in action, to see his method of approach, the way he cast a fly and where, to chart his success.

Anyway, he was curious as all hell.

He'd heard a great deal about this expert. We all have. He was the Fisher King himself, ready to lead us all to the Holy Grail.

So my friend parked himself uncomfortably behind the bushes and cravenly watched as the expert came around the bend, surveyed the long stretch of water before him, dipped thoughtfully into a large box of flies, chose his pattern, and began to fish. His casts were wondrously smooth; he laid the line out long and like a feather, probing the pockets and riffles deftly.

At first he caught no fish. My friend could not see if they were rising but he knew this stretch, knew it contained good fish, knew that on a June evening the browns should be rising to sulfurs. Nothing. The man pricked not one fish.

Then the expert changed his fly. Now, thought my friend, we'll see some action.

Again the line went out like a dream, and the skilled practitioner plied his art for a hundred more slow yards of gorgeous water. Nothing. Nothing even unto dark.

It had been a memorable performance, though, and my friend was glad he'd watched. Did it matter that the man had caught no fish? Not really. Not at all. Isn't one of the finest books of angling memoirs, by that grand legendary sparsely hackled angler, called *Fishless Days?* In it the author catches two barely legal fish. The expert had caught no fish, which did little more than affirm what we all know: Sometimes they won't be caught.

Back at the lodge, where the men gathered to swap flies and lies, someone asked the expert how many fish he'd caught that evening. Suddenly the chatter stopped. Not a glass clinked. Everyone, including my friend, turned to the famous man. Without a second's hesitation, the expert said, "Thirty-two."

Why?

Why did he feel compelled to tell such an outrageous stretcher? Would it have been so dreadful to say "Nothing" or "Not one" or "Skunked, most magnificently skunked?" I don't think so. In fact I can imagine that he would have given the others, who'd all taken a few that night, much pleasure to think they were a little more gifted than they'd thought. And would the expert's reputation have been diminished? Not the diameter of a 7X leader point.

And why did another expert feel compelled to have a local fish hawk catch and ice up some huge Western browns whole—so that when he got out there he could hold the fish up and have his picture taken with them for the magazines?

I happen to know and like these men, though I've fished with neither of them. I expect, sadly, that they were locked in by their expertise. No one was less free. They were condemned, like G. E. M. Skues's ill-fated Mr. Theodore Castwell, *always* to catch fish. What hell. And they had to do it; they weren't entitled to any more fishless days. What a pity. For aren't those days precisely what hook us most? Don't we remember most the big fish that we've lost, the days when the sweet mysteries of the river and its inhabitants eluded even our most sophisticated angling? Or perhaps it was not the cunning of the trout that made us fishless, but that we failed: Our timing was off, we were impatient, we missed our chances. What then? Twenty years in the classroom have taught me this much—we often learn most from failure, though few people have the heart to see it. Why should we hide our failures or fear them? They are the emblems of our humanity, beacons to what we yet may be.

Ah, dear. Preaching again. Isn't it all an attempt to justify my own admitted failings, to worm out of the embarrassment of putting flies in my ear and nearly falling on my assumptions?

Probably.

But at least if I am condemned *not* to catch fish, I am *free* not to catch them, either.

Still, there are times when the season is hot upon us, when I would like to get just a little more of the hundreds of miles of drag-free float the experts promise us; when I would like to know for sure whether the thorax tie will work best for a Hendrickson imitation; when I am more than a little curious about what the trout really sees; when I long for a bit of professional coaching and wish I could tie flies along the banks of a stream in my fingers. Like all of us, there are times when I would like to know just a little bit more.

As long as it doesn't interfere with my pleasure along the rivers.

This urge for privacy and pleasure and complete freedom from the connections that lead us to compete makes me a dismal friend along rivers. No sooner do I see moving water—its currents tangled and alive, its surface creased with the rings of rising trout—than I am lost, quite lost. The urge for expertness vanishes and I feel few of the juices of genial angling brotherhood well up inside me. I don't want to speak. I don't want to share my thoughts or my pool. I don't want to prove. I want no fishing friends, expert or not, near me.

I watch the water, then the world above and around it, make my calculations, and want to be quickly about the business of fishing. That's what I've come for, that and the solitude. If I take someone, I'm compelled to give him the best position in the pool—and to regret it all day—or not to give him the best position in the pool—and to regret it all day. Will he judge my casting? Shout when he raises a fish? Put down my fish? Breathe too hard? All manner of nasty speculations flood my mind.

This is my own problem, one happily that few fishermen share. Mike Migel, for instance, is a perfect saint along rivers. No sooner do we arrive at a new stretch of water than he directs me to the private haunt where the biggest, most generous old hookjaw is bound to be lunching that afternoon, and then he promptly retires to a rock, looks away, and begins a miraculously long and involved charade of putting new line on his reel, fussing with leaders, piddling with fly boxes (all of which, I swear, he arranged in perfect order in March, for he is a meticulous man). Worse, I've seen him make new friends along rivers—inviting perfect strangers to share whatever information he possesses.

This is all quite unintelligible to me, though I am forced to admit that I've been the glad recipient of such treatment.

But once off the rivers, once out of the maelstrom of quiet passion, I'm all ears. I can't get enough fish talk. And since I'm off considerably more than I'm on, I've discovered that a large portion of my delight in angling comes not on the stream at all or even in print, or even in tinkering with my tackle, but in talking or corresponding with friends who also love rivers. Some of them—among them my best friends— I've never even met.

Fish talk quickens a friendship, enlivens it with shared images and tales. Not long ago I visited Sandy Bing, an old friend who's vice-president in charge of research at a prominent stock-brokerage house. It was a busy afternoon for us both; I had some weighty questions to ask him about a subject light years removed from rivers, the Japanese electronics industry, and came full of the stolid queries that annual reports answer. I wanted to pick his brains in haste, then let him be about his affairs. But before we sat down, and scarcely having remembered that Sandy was not only an avid fly-fisherman but also the person who gave me my first bamboo fly rod (an exquisite seven-foot Thomas), I asked, half out of courtesy, "How was Montana last summer?" (Sandy has spent a month or more for most of the past thirty-odd summers in Montana.) And then, before he could answer, the thing began to form in my head, the image—deep inside, hungry—of certain Montana rivers: "I mean, the fishing. How was it? Were the rivers in good condition? Did you get any really big fish?"

How I brood about Montana! How deeply I am drawn there.

A half hour later he was still talking; in fact, he'd just gotten out some paper—there in his office, with secretaries and analysts trooping in and out, when we should have been discussing ADRs and Esaki Tunnel Diodes—and was mapping out a section of a certain spring creek he often fished. There was a huge bend pool, like so, with old aspens fallen in, right at the bend, and the currents worked this way and that— beyond the arrows I was beginning to *see* them—and you could only fish, obviously, from this spot, at point X. Obviously.

"Well, two fat browns were rising conspicuously at this precise section, letter O, and . . ."

"How big were they, Old San?"

"Oh, they were *big*, very big fish—five-pounders possibly. Maybe larger."

Five-pounders!

No sooner was the phrase out than I was there. Did he raise one? What were they feeding on? What fly did he use? How fine a leader point? Let's see. You had to cast from *here* to *here*—how far was that? Did he put enough snake in the line?

And so another half hour disappeared, and I didn't quite get all the proper weighty questions asked, and—alas—those two browns kept nosing up to a fly, then heading down and not rising for another ten minutes, confident as you please; then up they'd come again and start feeding, then refuse the fly again.

More than once, spurred by a chance image or phrase leaping at me from a crowded room, I have felt the strange shock of recognition and made a new friend. It takes one to know one. Some months ago I had a business lunch at the 21 Club and on the way out was introduced to Peter Kriendler, the owner. He is a professional host and greeted me warmly, then began to move away to other patrons. I had been lunching with the president of a publishing house and the general counsel for an international firm. "Nick's a fellow fisherman," said the president.

"You *fly* fish?" asked Kriendler, turning back. His eyes had widened, his voice became more intimate than required for the job.

"I have been known to," I said.

"Then you'll appreciate this," he said rapidly and launched into a long, wild tale about a salmon in Iceland, a rod that came apart at the butt, a reel that fell off while the salmon was on—all with appropriate animation and vigor. The president and the general counsel stepped back courteously, wordlessly—were they bored or frightened by this outburst?—as *the* rod was produced (an authentic visual aid), and the story continued until the salmon, improbably, was beached. I half expected to have *it* produced, too, in aspic.

But what is the source of that bond which makes us, in the best sense of that weary old phrase "brothers of the angle"? An expert I will never be, nor am I linked to a man by virtue of his expertise. There are other links. A golfer does not feel the connection with nearly the same intense familiarity as a fisherman does; after the handicap and the courses played and one's best game or shot are discussed, what's left? One grips his hands as if around a club, smacks an imaginary ball an old country mile, perhaps mentions that the Japanese write haiku about the sport—and then changes the subject. Nor do two sports fans want to do much more than acknowledge that they both saw the Oakland game last Sunday, or O.J.'s run, or Namath trying to run. Nor is the bond as sure and firm and intimate between businessmen, stamp collectors, skiers, Scrabble players, or even, necessarily, members of the same religion. Two Catholics, two Jews, or two Protestants who met and recognized each other as such would not quickly lapse into a discussion about the difference between Augustinian dualism and Thomistic reconciliation, Maimonides' *The Guide for the Perplexed*, or Channing's brilliant apology for Unitarian Christianity, now would they?

But two fly-fishermen, on short notice and with impassioned wit, may well discuss such sacred matters of practical piscatorial philosophy as the virtue of the thorax tie or the relative merits of Garrison and Payne rods; both may well have read the same Traver or Haig-Brown or Skues story, fished or wanted to fish a particular river. They would be interested in the esoterica of entomology—I have never fished in South America and probably never will, but the pancora crab and its imitation, and its effects on the growth rate of trout (they're ten-pounders in four years!) can capture my imagination for hours—and how to increase productivity in rivers. They will have favorite memories, cut from the gray fabric of humdrum days, that leap, fresh and green, from the mind of one to the common experience of them both.

Green thoughts, technology, triumphs, hilarious mishaps. Common and fascinating tackle (of great variety), a common language and a common and well-read literature, an inherent love of the vastly differing worlds of wild nature, an ethical base (increasingly concerned with matters of conservation), mysteries that are quite wonderfully unsolvable, or differently solvable, and so much more—these things surely bind us. Age and status don't count a whit. Among my closest fishing friends I number a twelve-year-old redheaded girl with freckles and pigtails and an intuitive love of rivers; a maverick twenty-eight-year-old movie maker; people in England, Maine, Montana, California, Bermuda, and Arkansas; mechanics; doctors; farmers; some guides; an expert or two; several octogenarians; professors in Chicago and Pennsylvania and Vermont and North Carolina. All but the fact that each of us is sweetly hooked on rivers vanishes.

Some of these friends I've never met, and one I now never will. Father Paul Bruckner, SJ, first wrote to me three years ago, after I'd sent him several books at the suggestion of a common friend and former student of his. I was told he'd been a magnificent English teacher at Marquette University for many years and had recently become quite ill.

Words flew from the doubting sinner in New York to that grand warm priest in Minnesota and back again, sixteen times. He passed shrewd and accurate judgment on some books I'd published, tested their theories with a steely Jesuitical logic against a knowledge of rivers he no longer fished.

He is gone now and I miss those letters—and the friendship. I don't know what he looked like, I never heard the sound of his voice, I did not listen to him teach Wordsworth or Newman or Waugh, but I shared a part of his life—rivers—an important part for us both, among the many parts we might have shared; and this meant much to us both. When I heard not long ago that—probably to keep from being a burden and expense to his brothers as he grew sicker and more dependent—he had shot himself (willing the worst for them), I wept. We had shared dreams and bright rivers and lore; we had been brothers under the skin.

Who will say we did not fish together?

Who will say we were not the closest of river-born friends?

3
A Catskill Diary

Go fish and hunt far and wide day by day—
farther and wider—and rest thee by many
brooks and hearth-sides without misgiving.
. . . There are no larger fields than these.
                    HENRY DAVID THOREAU

WE are finally settled in "Eastover," a weathered board
house at Byrdcliffe, high on the hill outside Woodstock. It is
an ample, dark- and pink-wooded house, built for the artist
Herman Dudley Murphy in 1903 by Ralph Radcliffe White-
head, that follower of William Morris who chose Woodstock
for his colony out of innumerable possible sites because of its
elevation and beauty. He had a theory that important art
could not be made at sea level.

Eastover is an artist's house, dominated by a massive studio
on the first floor with a thirty-foot ceiling, high windows, a
huge bluestone fireplace, a space oil-heater with rusted curv-
ing pipes; there is one small ash-stained chair, made by the
original craftsmen, and a shredding couch that we've placed
directly in front of the fireplace. Mari has set up her easel,
laid out her paints; I have stretched a half dozen canvases for
her, my one craft.

I have a small room for myself on the second floor and

have arranged my few books and papers and equipment. A whole summer! The first in more than fifteen years. From early June to September, with little to worry about other than the vastly complicated business of learning a bit more, as Yeats says, "to articulate sweet sounds together"—and finding some generous trout.

It is a vacation, I remind myself: respite, not removal. It is a chance to look more deeply, for a while, into rivers—and myself. It suits my growing misanthropy to be here, to be alone with my family. I have some private business to transact.

The town itself has grown chichi and is far more crowded than when we were here ten years ago. But it is isolated and quiet here on the hill, beneath the two huge maples. The house has wood sparrows in the eaves—there are fledglings in one nest—squirrels in the woodwork, two raccoons under the shed, two small rabbits that nibble on the large lawn, and a porch on which I have set up summer quarters for my tackle. I have hung my new waders on one nail, my old vest on another; I have laid out my leader spools and fly boxes and set up two fly rods. I have resolved to read the newspaper only once a week, the critics never, and to spend this one summer with my fly rods set up for the entire three months.

I fished only once this spring before we settled into East-over—that day on the Beaverkill in early May. I got to the No-kill section about noon, in good time for the Hendrick-son hatch that I knew had started several days earlier, took three very small fish on a nymph above Cairns's Pool, and kept waiting for the hatch to begin. About one thirty a few Hendricksons began to show but there was curiously no feeding to them. I stayed with the nymph, then tried, in succession, one of Art Flick's Red Quills (which have always been so successful for me), then Del Bedinotti's excellent tie of the Marinaro Hendrickson. Nothing. About three o'clock, when no fish had risen and none had been taken by the dozen or so other fishermen within sight, I switched impulsively to a huge Yellow Stone tied and sent to me by Charlie Brooks. I've had stone flies on my brain all spring. Sam Melner tells me that Walt Dette has a bottle of stomach contents of trout, and that 70 percent of the nymphs were stone flies; and I know they are in the stream all year long and represent the largest insect food available to trout. In the West they're taken for granted; here they're virtually ignored.

On my second cast, across and upstream, I had a sharp take as the fly swung below me. Really sharp. But I'd ignorantly not changed the light dry-fly tippet, and I broke the fish off. So I still have stone flies on the brain.

Then, about four o'clock, when I was about to give it up, I spotted the form of a large dark fish over a broad flat light-gray rock; it was high in the water, feeding. Then I saw another, and then another: long dark shapes, holding their positions. There were fifteen or so feeding freely now within my sight; they'd risen to just below the surface and were taking in that leisurely way I had seen trout rise on the Battenkill at dusk.

But rising to what?

At first I thought they had finally gotten a sweet tooth for Hendricksons, for there were still a few in the air, so I tried the Red Quill again on one of the nearest fish, a fourteen- or fifteen-incher. The fish rose an inch or two to inspect the fly, then drifted back; the second time I floated the fly past it, the fish didn't budge. I looked again. In the water and in the air I could see the telltale transparent wings of spinners; on the flat surface of the river they were like specks of mica.

Now the fish were lolling just under the surface, merely

tipping up, snouts out of water, and allowing the flies to drift into their open mouths. I had never seen this before, but if you spend enough time on rivers I suppose it's logical that you'll see more of what occurs, after its own laws, in moving water.

A No-Hackle with russet body and hen-hackle wings took five good browns for me, and I felt very satisfied with myself.

But on the way back I realized that I had been fishing in a bell jar, or fishbowl. However interesting the hatch itself, I was sharing that run with more than a dozen other fishermen, with the trucks to Binghamton that roared along Route 17, and with the thousands of other fishermen who had fished this popular run earlier in the season. I wondered whether the fish were really worth the loss of that part of fishing I value most—solitude. If you concentrate on a small patch of water and a few working fish, you forget all else—but isn't that an illusion? If the Catskills become very much more crowded, one will merely be going from "the desperate city," as Thoreau says, "into the desperate country."

The Esopus is the closest major river to Woodstock, and though it's never been a favorite of mine, I have reread Paul O'Neil's brilliant article, "In Praise of Trout—and Also Me," one of the finest profiles I know of any river. Perhaps I can renegotiate my uneasy détente with this river. It has always seemed inhospitable to me—a bit raw and rough and crowded—though before I fly-fished I used to catch hecatombs of trout in it.

I went upriver from Mount Tremper with Anthony tonight, to an old run I remembered from my teenage years. A lot of caddis flies were dancing on the surface, and a number of small fish were splashing for them. I tried a wet fly first but didn't get a tap. Then I switched to a small Gray Fox Variant—since the caddis were grayish—and raised several nine-inch rainbows. They were bright silver, bred in the river.

Anthony sloshed out to me without waders—since the spring, when he fell in, he finds it simpler to start wet—and I gave him my fly rod. The run is deep and fast, and I stood behind him and to his left, holding onto the bottom of his vest tightly, feeling him shiver in the cool June evening air. At first he slapped the fly down on the water brusquely, like a whip, but soon improved enough to take his first trout on a fly. It was a small fish, but he struck it well and smiled more brightly than the full moon as he reeled it in, almost to the tip-top guide.

On the way home, he was wet and shivering beside me. We sang "Summertime" and "The Battle Hymn of the Republic"—"Mine eyes have seen the glory . . ."—and saw, frozen in the headlights by the side of the road, a gorgeous amber deer.

Heavy, steady rains for two days. The Esopus is high and roiled. Worse, it is positively crammed with salmon-egg, corn-kernel, and minnow fishing fiends; this afternoon I counted fourteen of them in a stretch of river I had wanted to use to exorcise the stone flies from my brain. They were another breed. Is it snobbishness that I resent them? My fishing troubles them—and the river—not at all; theirs destroys mine and depletes the river. Anyway, I don't like the looks of them.

I have been learning the names of trees, weeds, birds, and flowers: sumac, locust, black walnut, ash, poplar, hickory, mountain laurel, whortleberry, rhododendron, anemone, finch, starling, bloodroot, marsh marigold, bluet. With names the eye sees more, in the fields and along the bright rivers.

One of my sons, studying for a college-entrance examination, is also learning words: plethora, derogatory, experiential, phenomenon, magniloquent, malevolent, conciliatory, concomitant, bemuse, garrulous, misogynist.

More rain. Art Flick—who lives over the mountain and has been inviting me over, when the weather is right—says he has never seen a worse season, either for gully washers or heavy heat and drought. He thinks the water will keep the rivers alive in the late summer, though. The portal at Allaben has been delivering surges of silt to the Esopus, which has been unfishable for a week.

You notice the weather more in the country. It has more of a direct link to your life. Everything is connected here. In the city, rain merely irritates.

Drove to Phoenicia, the same sleepy town it was twenty years ago; Woodstock has, by virtue of its name and the presence of large corporations near Kingston, expanded in a half dozen bad directions at once, and Hunter, because of its ski slopes, is radically changed from the tiny three-store town I knew as a child, when my grandfather owned the Laurel House in Haines Falls. I spent a few minutes with Herman Folkert and learned that his twin brother, Dick, makes those marvelous tear-drop nets, the best trout nets I know.

Reread Keats's poem "To One Who Has Been Long in City Pent" and found it true, not soft; and read Gauguin's *Noa Noa* and found this remarkable passage: "Civilization is falling from me little by little. I am beginning to think simply. . . . I have escaped everything that is artificial, conventional, customary. I am entering into the truth, into Nature."

But Woodstock is not Tahiti, I remind myself; and much, much of the Catskills is merely the desperate city transplanted, on vacation, its roads raw gray veins connecting major urban and industrial towns.

I have reread *Walden*, too, and found this passage. As Thoreau leaves John Field's house at Baker Farm and hurries off to catch pickerel, "wading in retired meadows, in sloughs and bog-holes, in forlorn and savage places" appears for an instant "trivial" to one "who had been sent to school and college." But then his Good Genius seems to say, "Go fish and hunt far and wide day by day—farther and wider—and rest thee by many brooks and hearth-sides without misgiving. . . . There are no larger fields than these, no worthier games than may here be played. . . . Through want of enterprise and faith men are where they are, buying and selling, and spending their lives like serfs."

And so I have gone off for a little while to play worthy games. I am not blind to the fact that I did not build the house I live in, that I use gas to cook on and gas to heat the house, that I have a telephone which connects me in an instant to Art Flick in West Kill or business associates in the city, that I travel to the rivers in a car and even use fly lines and leaders that are the product of modern technology, that the electric light permits me to read and write at night, that the plumbing carries away my wastes with a quick flush, that the food I eat is processed and packaged thousands of miles away, that the river I fish is not wild but merely a sluice between two reservoirs that supply the city with water, that this summer will cost me one hundred times what a whole year cost Thoreau, and that the trappings of modern society are not only part of my life here but conveniences I would not do without.

I find the notion of a permanent escape from the modern

world just that—an escape. A removal. It is not, I now see, what I want. In *Walden*, all radiates out from the pond, which could still be central. Today, ponds and rivers radiate from—and exist at the pleasure of—the cities. If the cities need their water, they will take it.

Even in *Huckleberry Finn*, which I have also reread, the river-shore dichotomy is misleading. Beyond the truism that there cannot be a river without a shore, the simple pleasures of the river take their meaning from what happens on shore. And, ironically, there is more vigor and wit and interest in the shore; the river is idyllic, removed, illusory, and, in permanent doses, dull.

Have begun to fish the Ashokan Reservoir for smallmouths nearly every evening at dusk. Still water is not flowing water, but it too has its appeal. Frankly, I don't know if smallmouths can be caught on a bug from the shore; I have asked no one, and no one else appears to fish this way. But I strongly suspect that fly-fishing for bass in reservoirs like the Pepacton and the Ashokan may be one of the great unexplored joys left in the beleaguered Catskills.

Anthony and several of his friends have been coming with me and are able to score well on wet flies for sunfish and rock bass. Last night Anthony took a gigantic crappie, a Moby Dick of all crappies—but he did not like its name.

The view from the Hurley Embankment where I fish is extraordinary, stretching back over the miles of the reservoir into the many layers of mountains. The sun breaks through the clouds at dusk far to the west and streaks down and infects the entire sky, like a medieval painting. The vast sky reminds me of Montana, where I have been lucky enough to fish several times, briefly.

But the Catskills are far, far from Montana. Why do I perpetually dream of other places? I am in the Catskills now; Montana will come later.

Drove with Mari along the pleasant, winding Route 212, then took routes 28 to 42, and over the mountains to West Kill and an evening of fishing with Art Flick. His hearty hello and unflagging vigor!

We immediately raced off in his car to the Schoharie, and he deposited Mari on top of a high rock embankment backed by the highway and overlooking the river and a spectacular patchwork quilt of meadows, farms, and hills. From far below, where I began to fish, she was small and practically camouflaged among the rocks as she began to work patiently on a watercolor.

I saw eight or ten fish come up, raised four or five on the small Gray Fox Variant Art advised me to use, and caught two.

About eight fifteen, a wind came up and Mari called down to me that she was cold. I had vowed to avoid the tragicomedies of my "fishing widow" days and decided simply that I'd had a good evening of it and would walk the three hundred yards upstream, then climb the rocks and give her my jacket. Art would be along before too long; he'd said he was only going a short distance downstream. But just then, a really huge hatch of *Potamanthus* began to emerge and the fish began to whoop it up royally. Up and down river, wherever I looked, the water was pocked by feeding fish.

The marriage or the trout. Not again!

What to do?

I hesitated and Mari called again, plaintively but not unfairly under the circumstances: she was perched on rocks in the near dark and was freezing.

I still had not made my decision and was watching an

especially bold riser that I could taste when Art drove up. "Stay where you are!" he shouted. "Stay as long as you want, Nick!" He'd left his favorite river in the midst of a major mayfly hatch, perhaps the first really good one he'd caught all this fluky year. A spectacular display of old-time chivalry. "Thought Mari might be cold," he called. "Don't hurry!"

So I didn't.

Fished the Esopus this evening a good distance above the Five Arches Bridge. Found a huge hole, the size and glory of a salmon pool, and raised two very acrobatic rainbows of perhaps fifteen inches each on a Dun Variant, just at dusk. There was twenty minutes of frantic feeding and the river was electrically alive with fish porpoising out of the whirling water, chasing the duns, but I could only raise those two and lost them both, one on a broken hook, the other on a pull-out.

If the Esopus could produce many evenings like this, maybe I'd stop dreaming about Montana.

What a pleasure it is to find such an isolated pool. I suppose, if one looks hard and long enough, there are still such places left, tucked into corners and away from roads. They are worth the exploring.

This afternoon was bright but cool, and after a shopping chore I explored several mountain brooks and finally stopped at the Little Beaverkill, an Esopus feeder and an old friend. The Esopus is unfishable *again* with the portal wide open.

A ten-inch brown was feeding regularly in the center of a small pool below a bend, and I naturally had my fly rod in the car, rigged with a Colorado King. I crept down the high bank onto a slate rock, made one long cast above the fish, and raised it—a bright jewel flashing, turning in the sun. I pricked it but no more, then made a half dozen fruitless casts and returned to the car.

Such brief, electric encounters are a simple, lasting joy this summer. They grace a day. They brush it with a touch of the wild. That fish will be there tomorrow, and next month, for me. And I now know four or five others—not large but native, I think—in the now-unfished Sawkill and Mink Hollow Brook.

But I won't tell you where.

To enlarge my day and gain more of the solitude I seek I have begun to fish the odd hours, and I have been thinking and dreaming more and more about nights and early mornings.

Clearly, the most fruitful time to fish, when you have the option, is when the fish are feeding. This summer I have that option. And the odd hours are providing special delights.

When I switched from worming and spinning for trout to fly-fishing, I was surprised to find how much pleasant midday angling was available: during the early spring (when I had usually fished from four to ten in the morning with worms), I discovered that the Hendricksons and Quill Gordons regularly hatched in the early afternoon, and later in the season that Cahills, Gray Foxes, March Browns, Cream Variants, a batch of different caddis flies, and much else came off, in their separate fashions, between midmorning and dusk. One could get out on the water late and be home reasonably early. Gentleman's hours. A family man's hours.

But I remember that very early morning—before more than a hint of sun was in the sky—was holy to me when I was a boy. Adults were sleeping, I often saw rabbits and deer in the meadows in summer, and—best of all—I had the lakes and streams to myself. There were always fish to be caught in South Lake near Haines Falls at that time, too, while the lake lay unruffled and shrouded in swirling mists. How well I remember walking down the mile-long road to the lake at five o'clock, listening to the scurry of little animals in the dark green woods around me, listening to the bright morning songs of the robins and jays and a dozen bright flitting birds I knew by sight but not by name. No one was at the planked dock, yet I would feel that the world around me was teeming with far more life than at midday, when scores of people jostled to get a boat and the noise was steady and raucous and raw.

Everything was fresh.

I had a twelve-foot fifty-cent bamboo pole in those days, and I attached heavy green cord to its tip, then a bobber, a short length of level leader, and a snelled No. 10 Eagle Claw hook. I carried my worms in the convenient Prince Albert tobacco can. When I swayed the bobber out into the lake, and the worm sank out of sight into the clear water, down into the channels between the lily pads, I had a sense of immediate attachment, a link firmer than steel to this lake.

You sat absolutely still and moved your rod not a millimeter. Your eyes were riveted to the bobber and wandered, dartingly, only when a wild duck came in with a splash or when a tawny spotted deer moved in the marshes where you often caught frogs. There were loons at the far end of the lake, and their cry was a stark and piercing call in the suspended dawn.

The lake belonged to itself and to its own creatures at this hour; while everyone else slept, this lake was singularly awake. There seemed ten times the number of perch and pickerel and pumpkinseeds in it before breakfast than after lunch, when the lake no longer belonged to itself but to the boisterous boaters and swimmers from the hotel.

When the red-and-white cork-and-quill bobber twitched, you froze. It bounced and bobbed for a few seconds, sending out circles, and you imagined some orange fish pecking and nosing around, down in its mysterious liquid world. Then, *zing!* it went down, and line shot out and you tugged sharply. If it was a large fish, you let it zigzag in circles for a few minutes before hoisting it in; most times you simply lifted, and a squiggling little sunfish flew out of the water and into the boat. Then you carefully ran your hand from head to tail to smooth and hold down the prickly dorsal fin, removed the hook, and tossed it back. Grandma would not cook sunfish— they were too small and bony—and you had already displayed enough full stringers at the hotel to know that such pride in one's catches was hollow.

When I caught a small silver shiner, I would hook it through the back and hunt for pickerel. Often in the early mornings when the lake was calm, I would take one of the oars out of the oarlocks and use it lightly as a paddle, gliding through the channels and peering into the strange green world below, where sometimes, when they were there, I could see the pickerel, long green solitary sentinels, suspended and unmoving along the edges of the pads. Waiting.

Then out would go the shiner, without a bobber this time, and I'd wait. The line would jiggle a little, twitch, move nervously and lightly. I would imagine the little shiner struggling feebly at the end of its tether. Then suddenly it would stop. That fish has got it, I'd think. Take it good. Take it down deep.

I'd wait, then wait a bit longer, then tighten up on the line ever so slightly. Then, in a rush, the fish would run off and I'd rear back and strike it just as hard as I could.

Those were golden mornings, etched individually and indelibly, "appareled in celestial light." And not the least of their appeal was that I lived them alone—before the world was awake.

Later, when trout fishing became my great passion and I could not wait until dawn to begin a new season, we broke in the new year at midnight and often took our legal limits of trout before sunup. But time and family and middle age happeneth to most of us, and for many years I forsook the cold dawn and late night for more sober and sensible and sociable hours. And I caught fish, especially when a hatch was on.

Now I am remembering the hard-won truths of my youth: Fish and most other wild creatures, for a variety of good reasons, prefer to feed and move about at the odd hours. Few creatures of the natural world like direct sunlight, which magnifies alarms, reveals them to their enemies, sends them into cover. And since most areas that are fished a lot, or are amply inhabited, present a lot of movement during the day, fish feel themselves safer when the human world is still. Perhaps most important, fish react poorly to heat: they feed less and grow lethargic. At night, or between the end of darkness and the first direct light of dawn, the water is cool. Safety, cover, and a temperature that sparks their hunger— these are the principal reasons the odd hours can be so fruitful, particularly during the late spring and hot summer months.

There are other good reasons, particularly for fly-fishermen. For one, a number of excellent fly hatches occur after dark and some continue until well after midnight. The great *Hexagenia limbata* in Michigan emerges at this time, and these mayflies draw some of the largest fish to the surface; the *Potamanthus* on the Battenkill provides fine fishing until nearly midnight. Moths, some of them huge, often fall into rivers at night and can provide a foraging old brown with a hefty mouthful. Field mice or voles move about at night and occasionally find their way into the water, and even frogs are more active. And the largest Eastern stone fly, *Perla capitata*, emerges in the last four hours before daylight on Catskill rivers; its nymphs become active several hours earlier and are prized by large trout.

I discovered night fly-fishing quite by accident. I was fishing a dusk hatch of a Cahill-like fly on the Battenkill one late June evening and found the fish rising vigorously just as the dark made it too difficult for me to change my fly easily. I did not carry any form of flashlight in those days, but since I could still barely make out the circles of rising trout I decided to fish a bit longer. The hatch had been disappointingly modest, but the trout were finally feeding freely. When I held my new fly, a large Cream Variant, against the light-dun sky to thread it, I saw something remarkable. I had thought there were few flies on the water, but above the dark line of the treetops—below which I could see nothing—the sky was clotted with enough large mayflies to make it look like a heavy snowstorm. There was enough of a moon for me to keep fishing without the aid of a light, and I fished until eleven thirty. The sky was still full of hatching mayflies when I left, all of which I would have missed—including the seven decent trout I took—if I had left the river at nine o'clock. One fish was a handsome seventeen-inch brown. The largest fish will often only feed after dark.

Art Flick had an interesting experience this spring. Mayfly hatches seemed, on the rivers he had fished, to be particularly sparse; yet he had several times found himself in the midst of a heavy spinner fall. When were the flies hatching? He theorized, and I think rightly, that with the great heat and a full moon the flies had been hatching at night and the trout gorging on them then.

These past weeks, though, I have preferred very early

morning fishing and think that in the summer this is the best time to fish. Water retains the heat of the day and takes many hours to cool. In the very early morning it is at its coolest, and I have found the fish active then.

This morning I got into the river at three thirty. The mists were heavy and the water intensely alive. I worked my way methodically downstream, fishing my big nymph across and down, feeling it sweep and waiting expectantly at the vital moment when it turned in the current.

There was a tap.

Then another.

The morning came in slowly, in silhouette, changing the forms of brush and trees and hills from an amorphous gray to sharper black and then to their true colors; the light keenly etched all forms and a symphony of bird sound and water began. The air was chill and fresh. Best, for me, was the solitude. Who else would be fool enough to fish at this hour?

Another cast across and downstream. Then another. Ten. Twelve. Twenty casts. Maybe fifty. More. Suddenly the bright river exploded. A rainbow took, when the fly hesitated and rose to the surface, and then came crashing up, jumping once, twice, and careening downstream.

The sun signaled its arrival and then leaped, too, over the foothills—bright, dazzling the eye.

I like fishing *into* the daylight rather than into the deepening dark. When you're done, the day is awake and the river dead; I am never quite sure that I have not left too early when I fish at night, and too long in the hooded dark on a large river is bad for my nerves.

Fishing the odd hours expands my options, allows me to see the same rivers differently. These are witching hours. When the rest of the world is snugly asleep, I find that rarest quality of our day, solitude, and the rivers can be magnificently alive.

I waded the rocky shores of the Ashokan at dusk tonight, casting a small popping bug as far as I could, as the ruffled lake calmed down and the sun dipped below the ring of mountains, mauve to lighter mauve. When the bug landed, I let it lie a few moments, then raised my rod tip in short twitches to plurp it along the surface, as I had learned to do last September in Maine.

Suddenly there was a swirl and I felt a firm tug. A good smallmouth. It came up once, twice, then again, shaking high—a really fat, strong fish.

And then it was off.

So there *are* smallmouth to be caught here on bugs! I'll fish it all summer now, whenever—as has been the case for another four nights this week—the Esopus is unfishable.

I drove to Manhattan and back today for some business and could feel the tension mount the moment I left the West Side Highway. Traffic jams. Arrogance and hatred in the streets. Corrosive politicking at the office. In the newspapers, clever men crying the catch-cries of the clown. The same crew on upper Broadway in the early evening. This place on the hill is not Walden Pond or Tahiti, but it permits certain values to be maintained, husbanded—electric lights notwithstanding. Here I can choose as much of the modern world as I want to partake in my life and exclude the rest. There is no fallacy in taking some, in riding the railroad rather than allowing it to ride you. The electric light does me no harm; it enables. So does the stillness of the night and the grass, woods, and view from my window here.

The hot, heavy days of mid-July have started, but there's still a lot of water I want to explore. Len Wright has given me "poaching privileges" on his upper Neversink water, above what's left of Hewitt's old section of the river, and I'll probably go over later in the summer. And I will want to try the Beaverkill and Willowemoc, very early in the morning or perhaps at night, and perhaps the East Branch (if those bastards who control the water flow will let in cold water), the upper reaches of the Rondout, and more of those small, cool, clear mountain brooks. Sparse has invited me for a day on his DeBruce Club water, and that's always a joy. I have my dreams. Somewhere, mingled among them, is a wish to return to the Laurel House, which more and more takes the shape of a spring from which so many of my waters flow.

In June our fat raccoon appeared one evening, slimmer and with three "gray fox" babies; one looked frail and now there are only two little ones. The fledgling wood sparrows are gone. Did the raccoons get them? There is life and death, Darwinism in action, a bit of the untamable, all around me. My rods, a No. 5 for trout and a 6 for bass, are still always fully rigged, on the porch or in the car. Ready.

The Sawkill heads in Echo Lake, near Overlook Mountain, flows through a backwoods valley lush with birch and poplar, crosses Route 212 at Shady, turns with the road at Bearsville, and then winds down past Woodstock, through the golf course, toward Zena. Much of the upper water is small and posted, but I have fished the five or six miles between Shady and the eastern edge of the golf course, every pool and run of it, many times in the past. The Sawkill is always a genial, clear, underfished creek, rather small and growing smaller each successive day of the summer; some years the water simply vanishes—slipping between the rocks to some underground shelf and leaving small, unmoving, stagnant pools.

At its best, ten years ago, it provided a pleasant evening's spot-fishing for ten-inch browns, with always the chance of moving a holdover of some size on a delicate cast to some deeply undercut bank. I once found an eighteen-incher locked in a small bend pool—and raised it three times, its rise explosive in such small quarters.

Not a little of my interest in spending a summer in Woodstock was the thought of the Sawkill just down the hill. So when we arrived in early June I picked out a calm evening and went to a back-section I knew. The cream-colored dorotheas were on, and I took seven fish up to twelve inches in little more than an hour. I released the fish and returned to Eastover elated: I would have fish all summer, and the river to myself, since I remembered seeing few fishermen on it after May.

Wrong. When I tried the creek on a drizzly day several weeks later, a half dozen teenagers were fishing the section on which I had caught the dorothea hatch; they were using live minnows, about an inch long, and three of them had a dozen trout, hung by strings from their belts. They had cleaned it out.

And as I fished that day, and others, up past other sections I remembered with affection, I saw that extensive bulldozing had flattened the streambed and that there were now many more houses near the banks. The little creek could not bear such pressure.

So I did not fish it again until this afternoon, a hot, bright, mid-July day. The family decided to go swimming about two o'clock. Fine. But I bathe in other waters. I was off to explore a section of the Sawkill I had not fished yet this season, that I remembered holding up well in the summer. Ten years ago you could take some nice browns, even on such a bright July afternoon as this, on a No. 18 Hairwing Royal Coachman. I remembered the way the bright little fly danced down the clear rapids, the take of a foot-long trout, a barracuda in these waters. I remembered the surprises in this section that year: that eighteen-incher, and specific thirteen- and fourteen-inchers hidden back in the root-tangled pools and undercut banks that the town kids had been unable to fish out in May.

My rod was in the car, set up; I had only to add a length of fine tippet and the small ocher Colorado King that has been working so well for me. No boots today—just my vest and old fish hat, and then a bit of quick mountain-goating down the rocks to the streambed.

But the stream was far different from the brisk water I had fished when the dorotheas were on, or ten years ago. The flattened bulldozed pools were long shallow runs with only several inches of water in them now. There was no visible holding water and I was convinced, even before I cast, that there were no fish. Still, the little rock-strewn creek with its dancing spring water—cool, sparkling, clear—was better than the public swimming pool with the name of Swim-o-Links. There might still be a lesson or two to be caught here— a sound, shadow, image I might creel forever.

I fished downstream first, using ten-to-fifteen-foot spot casts into the head of the diminutive riffles, watching the fly dance down into the slicks. The spring water seeped into my old sneakers and was cold. My face perspired heavily, and I had to take off my sunglasses and wipe them clean. The creek was a major river in microcosm—but without fish.

There was nothing downstream but a few pecking dace, so I headed up, moving quickly, hopping along the rocks, most often keeping a short length of line moving in the air even when I was not fishing. I found a larger pool and put one cast into its tail. Nothing. Another at the base of the riffle. Nothing. One into the head of the riffle. Yes—only no. A dace.

At the bridge I spotted my first trout of the day, a quick

darting shadow. It had been resting beneath the rock in the tail of the pool and, after darting back and forth, settled beneath the little boil of falls and foam. A sensible choice for a hot afternoon. I knew I couldn't take it then but decided to come back that evening or early the next morning. I knew I could take that trout easily after a careful approach at the right time of day.

Better yet: I won't fish for you at all, old last Mohican.

I have found pockets and patches of the serenity I expected in the Catskills—a pool on the Esopus, the headwaters of a few feeder creeks, a run on the Schoharie—but year by year they too are encroached upon. Where I remember a pleasant meadow, there's a garish shopping center; where I fished an isolated stretch of river, a superhighway now skirts its path, and the river can never fully come back now for the cars will always, in increasing numbers, rowel your ears. I fished such a run at three o'clock one morning—and the cars still came by every minute or so.

Kurt Vonnegut recently told some graduating seniors that things are rotten and are going to get worse. "Some men, like bats, have eyes for darkness only," says Dickens in his marvelous *Pickwick Papers*, disclaiming such eyes, at least there. One surely does not want to be so, but even on this pleasant hill, this pocket of quiet patrolled by oak, maple, and pine, within twenty minutes of five rivers, it is hard to avoid that ocular disease.

A number of unpleasant episodes that I hope are not auguries of innocence permanently lost. Last night on the Ashokan, just when I got my first strike, some overgrown no-neck monsters began to set off firecrackers and toss cherry bombs at the car in which Mari was reading. There were a dozen of them, drinking beer, shouting threats, and they scared her half to death.

Then tonight, with the Esopus high, I went up near Shandaken and found a pleasant run with eight-to-ten small rainbows rising playfully in it. I had taken one when a green apple the size of a golf ball hit the water in front of me. I thought it might have fallen from a tree but there was none nearby. Then three or four others, in rapid succession, pelted into the water or against the rocks. Some kids had to be throwing them, but they must have been behind the bushes up near the road for I couldn't see anyone. I thought they might not know I was there, so I simply waded downstream, but the pelting followed me. I breathed deeply, then shouted; the apples kept coming. Finally I crossed the river, climbed the bank, and saw half a dozen of them standing up the road beneath an apple tree, cackling like daws, leering. One of them had been serving as point man, directing their fire. When he saw me he raced across the road, and all of them scurried behind a barn. Like chickens.

Both incidents recalled that eerie story Mike told me, of his being caught midstream in the heavy Saranac River and having rocks thrown at him by four leather-jacketed motorcyclists. One of them had shouted, "Let's give Pops a lesson"—Mike is over sixty—and they headed into the river after him. He was several miles back in the woods, waist deep in strong current, standing on slippery rocks. He had feared for his life.

Sooner or later, probably sooner, the mad world will fully find every corner of our gentle rivers where we pursue—to no one's harm and our quiet joy—this simple passion. It is hard at times like now not to have eyes like bats.

In the Pepacton, at night, the men fish with lanterns hung from the ends of their boats, lowering huge sawbellies to depths of thirty and forty feet. This is an exotic sight on a trip back from the Beaverkill, but I cannot imagine I would enjoy fishing that way—even for the ten-pound browns that are regularly extracted.

Is there no way to fish for them with flies?

In Henrys Lake, small shrimp and damselfly imitations take trout up to seventeen pounds. I should like, one whole season, to explore the Pepacton with streamers, large nymphs, bass bugs, and Thom Green's Leech. I'm sure big bass and some of the larger browns can be taken on a fly.

But then, I'd like to spend a whole season doing other types of fishing much more, and in other places. In the night, despite all my vows not to think of other rivers, I often dream of the Yellowstone and the Firehole and Henrys Fork of the Snake and other rivers of the West—and sometimes of one truly gigantic trout I once hooked, and lost, in Henrys Lake.

They are a long way from here.

I have just returned from my second trip to the upper Neversink. The ride over Slide Mountain at Big Indian and Oliverea is memorably beautiful and still wild, and the water I fished is exquisite. But the fishing both times was poor.

The Wright water, a bit less than a mile of it, is just above the Big Bend Club, and the land is lush with thick wild rhododendron and pine, and juicy—with several springs and several spring-fed creeks delivering their cold water to the main river constantly. The stretch has every conceivable kind of water—ledge pools, riffles, bend rapids, flats, glides, pockets, and undercut banks—and has been improved judiciously with siding and riprap. It is cool all summer, all one could want of a trout stream.

The first time I went I took some small brookies and one small brown; the second time, with Bill and Dorothy

Humphrey, I merely got two slap rises from tiny brook trout before we were rained off in midafternoon.

We picnicked on a spit of land under the pines, overlooking one of the creeks, on cantaloupe and tomatoes from the Humphreys's garden, and on Dorothy's tuna casserole—and then walked downstream through the tangles to the bottom end of Wright's water. There were deer tracks everywhere. Bill and I saw five trout, in formation, in a backwater—all of them about fifteen inches—but the water was so low and frighteningly clear that we could not move them. The best fish moment of the day was watching Bill raise a brown in the current of the ledge pool. That electric flash!

I have been studying, for several hours each day, a rich, complex, and difficult book called *The Ecology of Running Waters* by H. B. N. Hynes. This is my first exposure to scientific works on rivers—or science of any substantive nature, except for piscatorial entomology—and it is deeply revealing. Watching rivers now, I see more of the many physical laws that are their fiber and bone and blood. "A river channel," says Hynes, "is thus an almost infinitely adjustable complex of interrelationships between discharge, width, depth, rate of flow, bed resistance, and sediment transport. Any change in one tends to be countered by adjustment in the others, and the whole system tends towards conservative dynamic equilibrium." I like that last phrase. It explains much.

Nor does science in any way spoil my pleasure, as at times I feared it would. It scarcely troubles me that ichthyologists consider my lovely trout a "low form" of fish. The job was done right the first time, and the *fact* of it supports my general and increasing scepticism toward the new and the novel.

I always knew that all rivers were different; it is good to learn from science that they overlap.

We drove to Haines Falls last week, to the Laurel House, where I caught my first fish in the weedy lake and gigged the first trout I ever saw, beneath the bridge over the unnamed mountain creek.

The main road is three-lane—it had barely been two, and rough macadam then—and new motels and restaurants have sprung up everywhere. Ski madness has hit the remote valley and new, fashionable condominiums and chalets festoon the hillsides, built of dark wood, each with its own terrace and fireplace—a bit of mock Switzerland grafted onto this back-water Catskill valley that once supported only small, modest, family resorts.

"Is there anything to do there?" my son asked as we turned off the highway at the little old church, exactly as I had remembered it: tawny wood-slab sides, white shutters, the pretty garden in front, behind the picket fence.

I remembered that I had always had too much to do at the Laurel House. The days were too short. Every minute was crammed with some game or discovery. I would be up at five, with the first touches of light, and down at the creek or on the lake. I began to see my white-bearded grandfather, whom I loved, sitting in front of the little cottage off to the left of the hotel in the cool evenings, reading the *Daily Forward*; the orchard across the creek and up to the left; the creek I tramped daily, catching untold numbers of crawfish and frogs and tiny bright trout that skittered and flopped in your hand like long spotted jumping beans; the long walk to the lake in the early mornings, when slants of sun broke through the heavy pines and hemlocks and my heart was light and open and pounding like mad.

You think at such moments of the bends your life has taken, the course of the river from there to here, then to now, from its simple source to who knew what. How because you were very young and your stepfather was a cold fish and a martinet, you studied business at college, "so you'll always have it," then switched abruptly after the army years to English; how you wanted to write—that most of all—but taught and edited and then wrote other people's books for them; the editor had said you were the fastest and best ghost in the East, which he meant to be a compliment. Small apartments, many children, debts that covered your heart like weeds, barbed wire through your veins, senseless bickering. Now you did not edit any more and did not ghost and would not be teaching for much longer either, though you loved your students. This was a year for a new beginning and this was a long summer, and we were going back to the Laurel House. It would be good to see the old hotel, where the river took its source.

"Are you sure this is the right way?" Mari asked.

The sides of the road were pocked by cheap shacks and trailers—little tinny worlds inhabited by sloppy people. There were thirty or forty on little half-acre plots where there had been only two houses on the road thirty years ago: a neat clapboard cabin, rarely occupied, and that old Victorian spook house I had once climbed into with my cousin. We were where the cabin had been and I had not seen it as we went by; the foundation of the old mansion was up on the left, a trailer on either side of it now. "This is positively ugly and slummish," Mari said. "It looks like they've moved half of upper Broadway up here. You said it was isolated, covered with blueberries that you picked on the way to town."

"It was."

"Is this where you used to ride on the running board of someone's old truck?" my son asked.

"Joe's. The handyman."

"God, that must have been fun."

"It was."

After we passed the ruins of the old Victorian house, its chimney stack halfway broken off, its shrubs run wild, I recognized nothing. Maybe Mari was right. Maybe, somehow, I had taken a wrong turn. It could happen. I had taken wrong turns before. Those ruins might not even have been the building I remembered; they might have shifted the course of the road. I slowed to twenty, then fifteen miles per hour. There had been a view, I remembered, of the surrounding mountain peaks; I would often pause, with my cousin, and look at it on the walk to town. The trees now so overhung the road that I felt I was driving in a tunnel.

"Can I get a strawberry cone when we get there, Dad?"

"Sure," I said, abstractedly. There was a canteen in the basement of the hotel. We could buy the ice cream there.

I scrutinized each dirt road on the right now, looking for that familiar turnoff with the swinging sign mounted on the cedar-log frame. There had been no other roads off to the right. That entire side of the road, all the way to within a quarter of a mile of Haines Falls, except for the cabin, had been wild, filled with low blueberry bushes that I had plucked in August, tangled raspberry and blackberry vines clustered thick among the low birches and alders and towering oaks, dark mountain laurel shrubs with bright pink flowers in June—and always the view, stretching across the deep valleys to the far mountain ranges, cobalt and mauve on a lazy late-August afternoon like this.

"Laurel House Road."

Even at fifteen miles per hour I almost missed the foot-long sign, and the dirt road, which looked exactly like so many of the others. I felt a flutter in my chest. I could not wait to see the old place, walk several of my old trails, across the nine-hole golf course where the blackberries would al-

ready be ripe; down the hill to the swimming pool, with that
silver-green creek, always icy cold and clear, behind it. I
didn't even know its name but I was ready to bet anything I
could remember every rock of the place where I had gigged
my first trout. Perhaps I'd take my son on the path to the lake
or down to the famous falls behind the hotel, where I had
carved my name among so many others on the big flat rock. I
always remembered the place scene by scene: a particular
morning on the lake; the night of my grandparents' fiftieth
wedding anniversary, with those glorious swans of ice I had
watched being carved in the afternoon and the platters of
cold cuts and bowls of fruit, and my grandfather, still stern
but with happy glossy eyes, a patriarch there on the dais, surrounded by hundreds of his friends and relatives. He was
dead now. I saw few of my relatives. I had slept until eleven
thirty the next day, after the midnight supper, and my cousin
and I had talked about it for weeks.

Memories had mingled with affections, becoming so much
a part of the fabric of my bone and blood that they often had
to be pried loose, one by one. I could see the large white-
pillared hotel itself, as clearly as if it were yesterday, with the
circular drive and the ring of lilac bushes that were always in
full bloom when we came up each June; the back porch
where my uncles, with great hairy chests, played pinochle in
the sun; the tire swing and compost pile behind the kitchen,
where I dug worms for bait; and the old bridge across the
creek and the barn with its cows and huge silver milk cans,
and my grandfather in the shed, whacking the heads off
chickens he seized mercilessly from a jammed wooden cage,
feathers flying furiously—blood on him, on me, on the saw-
dust floor.

Mostly I remembered the lake and the creek. I remembered everything starkly but piecemeal; I couldn't quite put

the parts or the years together—when what happened, where it all stood in relation to everything else. But I remembered, in careful sequence and unchanging image, the lake and the creek and all the times I had become a part of them.

Was that why I wanted to come back?

Did I really think I could recapture something I had at this place, at that time when all the world was young, now gone perhaps forever?

I raced the car as I made the sharp turn down Laurel House Road and felt the wheels skid on the dirt and the car swivel.

"Nick!"

"I've got it. Don't worry. I remember the place now. This is the right road. I've got everything under control. The golf course is just around the second bend."

"Can we play, Dad? Can we? I hit golf balls last summer, on that range in Connecticut, and you said I was terrific. Can we, Dad?"

But there was no golf course around the second bend. When we came past the turn I saw only a lightly wooded field. The grasses were over two feet high, I could see no mounds that might have been greens, and the entire area was so sprinkled with trees—some of them four and five feet high—that it was impossible to conceive where a golf course might ever have been.

"Where's the golf course?" Mari asked.

"I don't see a golf course, Dad."

"It was . . ."

"You promised we could play, Dad. You promised."

"I did *not* promise."

"Are you sure you got the right road, Nick?"

"I am quite sure," I said, my voice taking on an edge, "that I took the right road."

Poplars and birch, four or five feet tall, rose out of the high grasses. If there had been greens, neatly trimmed, they were long gone. There had been a small clubhouse where, after the season, I had often found golf balls, tees, a broken club or two, some small change. In the lower corner of the field, near the road, there was now no structure.

Huge logs blocked the main road, so I stopped the car, got out, and walked to where the clubhouse had stood. I bent over. Nothing. Only thick shrubs, sproutlings, high grasses.

"You'll love the view from the falls," I told Mari, my voice beginning to rise slightly. "It's right in back of the hotel. I once carved my name in the rocks—my real name, before my mother remarried. It's just a short walk around the bend and down the hill. Behind the hotel."

We walked, the three of us, slowly down the hill. I told my son how the old barn had stood over to the right, near a huge patch of blueberry bushes. There had been four milch cows and hundreds of chickens whose stock was replenished weekly by a truck that came with dozens of wooden cages on it, crammed with squawking white birds fated for the hotel dining tables. I held my son's hand, put my arm lightly around my wife's shoulder. From the condition of the road, the neglect of the golf course, and the logs across the path, I knew the hotel—already a hundred-year-old relic when my grandfather owned it—would be unused, neglected, fallen into disrepair, but it would be good to see those large white pillars, the great circular drive, the old porch in back, that world that had been my childhood, every long summer from before memory until I was thirteen.

Suddenly I wanted to share it all with my son. I wanted this place not only for myself but for him, with whom I quarreled too much, knew too slenderly, loved.

The boy was quiet. He held onto my hand tightly.

We turned the bend in the road—and it was not there.

I looked down into the hollow where the hotel once stood and saw only a tangle of high grasses and brush, small poplars, birch, and pines. There were half a dozen mountain laurel bushes; there was no hotel.

"Where is it, darling?" asked Mari.

"It was right there."

"Where?" asked the boy.

"There, there," I said, pointing. "Don't you see?"

"Nope."

"I'm afraid I don't see anything either, Nick."

"They tore it down. That's all. But the foundation will be there. I'll show you."

We walked more quickly now, down into the hollow which, on a Fourth of July or Labor Day, once teemed with people I knew, many of them family: uncles, aunts, cousins, second and third cousins, friends of my uncles and aunts whom I also called "uncle" or "aunt," my grandparents. There would be old Dodges and Buicks parked in the road that led to the falls; children playing in the sandbox behind the back porch; that interminable pinochle game; dozens of people in the circular driveway, talking, laughing, heading up the hill to play golf or to the old concrete swimming pool; people arriving and hugging old friends; people chatting with animation, laughing at some old story, of which there were hundreds. I knew all the people; the same ones came back every year and I was related, somehow, to every one of them. They were all "family."

I ran the last forty yards down the hill alone and was walking now on the ground on which the hundred-room hotel had stood. Nothing. Boulders. Wild grasses. Several clumps of tiger lilies. Saplings. Clumps of high weed. Brambles, tangled and untended. I thought I remembered where the

neat grove of lilac bushes once stood, off to the right. In a
cluster of thirty or forty trees, I saw three, past their bloom. I
walked slowly over the humps in the ground, pushing away
the high timothy and weed with my feet, looking down at the
roots of all this dense growth for some specific sign, any sign,
that this was exactly where the hotel had stood. I found
none. The land was wild. There was not one indication, anywhere, that the Laurel House or any other human structure
had stood in this place.

Only the falls were still there—the flow less than I remembered it, but the same crystalline creek, flowing out of the
heavy pine and hemlock forest, down over slate-bottomed
pools, over the great cleft and down into the awesome clove.
The space stretched out, and then farther out and down, and
I felt the hollow twinge in my loins which I had always felt
when I was a boy and played too close to the brink of this
ledge, and the three of us looked silently out across the il-
limitable space, across the clove, toward the intersecting
mountains in the far distance, cobalt and mauve and Payne's
gray, layered, textured, growing dimmer as they stretched
back farther and farther into the distance until the eye could
see them no more.

Later we searched the rocks for my name but could not
find it among the hundreds of others; perhaps the water, in
spring torrents, had washed it away. I had been ten years old
when I scratched it into the stone and perhaps had not dug
deeply enough. We walked up the creek toward where I had
caught my first trout. We could not reach it. The forest had
claimed its own. The entire hollow had returned to some
primitive state. It was as if nothing from my past existed at
all, as if, were I to build here, ever, I would have to start, not
from family or hotel but from the rocky earth, the maze of
brush tangles beneath my feet, the same bright creek flowing
out of the wild forest.

Auguries of autumn: The day is bright and warm in the late morning and afternoon, but about five o'clock a coolness enters the air that has not been present since May. Is it different in itself or only in contrast to the recent summer heat? It *feels* of autumn; it has the tang and hue of the fall, though there is still a week left of August. Last night darkness came by eight fifteen. This morning I turned on the space heater. The trout will begin to move soon; the smallmouths will surely be up out of the depths more regularly now.

The blast of cold these past few days of early September brought with it the sure shiver of recognition: summer is nearly over. The time to return is nearing. I cannot resist counting—and trying to hold back—the few days left. Brief patches of red and red-gold on some oaks and maples; pale orange splotching the birch.

Rain all day. An icy up-country rain, in gusts. Impossible to fish. So I have been trying to reconstruct that fall day two years ago when that awesome brown appeared.

The sumac was already maroon that day and birches scattered throughout the pine hills blazed orange and red. "Fall is the time of movement," said Roderick Haig-Brown, and you could see movement and change everywhere. Oak and maple were changing. Cattail stalks in the marshes were sere and lovely and still. The season was changing, too, from trout to no-trout time. And I was driving upstate for a last restful day of it before returning to the long gray city winter.

I knew the satisfactions of this season: the somber solitariness of the rivers, the need to hunt your fish, to probe the usually shrunken water; skies a blue blaze and leaves an unthinkable rose; the air sharp, enlivening, even severe, with more than a hint that snow would come soon. The smaller fish seem to be gone, the stockers are wiser, there are fewer fish and the larger ones are shoring up for the winter on big food.

Maybe there was one more day to be squeezed, like Keatsian cider, from the season; maybe not. I had my expectations.

I got to the Catskill river after two. The afternoon was mild, sunny; perhaps I would move a fish or two, perhaps not. Did it really matter this time? Nothing—certainly not a fishless afternoon—could spoil the "mellow fruitfulness," the fullness of this late-autumn day. I had not even taken waders. Why go through the drill? It would be pleasant enough, this time, simply to cast from that wide gravel bar, where there was ample room for a backcast. I would stay dry and warm and comfortable, which fitted my mood.

I threaded the line through my fly rod carefully, sitting on a rock and watching several rise forms that made lovely spreading circles in the slick glide, following the length of the run with my eyes right up to the head of the pool, where I intended to fish last. There was no hurry. I ran the leader through a square of rubber three, four times, until it was carefully straightened; I ran its length through my mouth twice, to dampen it. I tied on a Hairwing Royal Coachman slowly, tested the knot, clipped off the excess stem of the leader with my clippers.

Then I picked out the nearest circle, positioned myself, and cast to it. An immediate strike: a small chub. Another three casts: another chub.

The water was warm. Had the trout remained in the spring holes, where they'd been all summer? Most likely. The whole stretch might be barren. The water was too warm for late September, too low. If there were trout here, they'd have to be at the head of the pool, in the deep hole below the riffles, where—I could see—the water was still fast and choppy.

I reeled in and headed slowly upstream, watching the water and the blaze of orange leaves and a few waxwings high above the alley of the stream, circling.

I saw a gray-tan grasshopper among the rocks and decided to change my Coachman for a Hopper. I had one left. There were a few circles in the pool, where the current flattened. It was a lovely, peaceful afternoon, and I knew I would not be disappointed if I only took a few more plump aldermen. Slow, cottony clouds. A soft light-blue sky. A certain crispness inside the mild autumn breezes. The river to myself. The pleasure of feeling the line move comfortably, cleanly, in the air—for I was casting better than I had that spring.

A chub slapped at the Hopper but did not take. I cast up into the current three more times and hooked a frisky small-mouth of about ten inches, which jumped a few times and fought hard until I brought it close and slipped the hook out of its mouth. Smallmouths would be enough. If that's all there was, surely I'd take them. Another inch or two in size and they would be more than enough action for a day like this.

Then I saw a little spurt of water at the head of the current. I felt a flutter in my chest, a quickening.

I checked the fly and leader, then cast five feet past the spot where the fish had risen. The fly glided swiftly, up and down on the little wavy riffle. There was a small splash rise, I struck, and then the huge fish leaped and came down and then rolled and leaped again and then bore upstream into the heart of the run, toward the jutting rock.

I reacted quickly.

I took several quick steps upstream, holding the rod high, and tried to keep the fish from gaining the eddy below the rock. It got into it for a second, two seconds, and then the current forced it up and out into the mainstream again. It'll go below me now, I thought. It was a huge trout, nineteen inches, perhaps—and heavy. If it runs, I'll follow it, I thought.

But the fish didn't run; it bore deep into the center of the pool, and I knew then that I had it. It would no longer have the strength for a sustained run, and the current was not strong enough to help it. I waited and pumped steadily, firmly, and in a few minutes the fish was up and coming toward me. It was a splendid, brightly colored male, native born, I guessed, and soon I had it in the net.

I sat down again, took out a pipe, and breathed deeply. A lovely day. A splendid, quiet, plump-joyous day. Some excitement—a bonus. It had not been necessary but I had enjoyed taking the big brown. It was a good fish any day. Perhaps now I would just watch the water for another ten minutes and then head out to the car. It had been a perfect hour. I probably would not move another trout if I fished until midnight, and if I did it would be anticlimactic. I'd had enough excitement for one afternoon.

I watched the moving water and the trees, the poplar leaves shimmying as if they were on ball bearings. A smallmouth jumped once, twice, three times in succession downstream, perhaps chasing one of those mahogany duns I now saw; there were a few tempting rises near the opposite bank. They *might* be trout. No matter. I had had enough.

Well, maybe another half-dozen casts. I had the time. Then I would make my final, reverent good-byes and head back toward the long city winter.

On my first cast I hung the Hopper high in a willow. I tugged lightly at the line a few times and, when the fly would not come free, went to the tree and tried to reach the branch to which the fly was hooked. I could not quite make it; the branch was five, six inches too high. Did I have to make that last cast? I tugged steadily several times, then yanked. The leader snapped back at me without my last Hopper.

I poked around in my fly box for a few minutes, found nothing I liked, found another box, and settled for a gargantuan fly I had never used before. It was a skater the size of a cue ball, and its hackles had been bent by a compartment too small for it. I scarcely thought I would catch anything with it, but I had never tried a skater that large and it would ride well in the heaviest current, where I could see it plainly.

I cast a dozen times with care, watched the huge puff of hackle ride the waves, and then lost interest. A couple of waxwings were in the trees across the stream, and for a moment I watched them hop from branch to branch, while letting a long cast play itself out downstream. One of the birds flew off. I hoped I could see it take one of the few mahogany duns still coming off the water. The bird flew high, then banked—and then I heard a tremendous splash across the stream, flicked my head, saw it was at my fly, yanked, felt the turn of a really huge fish . . . and broke it off.

My right hand was shaking.

A slight tremor worked its way into my legs.

My chest heaved from the pounding. A big fish. A really big fish. Four pounds? Maybe. Damn! I kept watching the spot, hoping the fish would jump, as they sometimes do, to shake the hook. No. It was too big. It had felt a hook before. It would not jump and it would not rise again. Damn!

I took a step back and looked at my leader, parted at the first knot. Stupid, blundering ass. Idiot. Why the hell had I reared back? Gone. Won't come back. Best fish of the year and I act as if I never had a fly rod in my hands. Idiot. Haven't done a fool thing like that all year. Did I *have* to watch those miserable birds?

The shaking had not stopped; my chest was still heaving.

"Gone. It won't rise again. Not today," I muttered out loud, biting hard on the stem of my pipe. My voice sounded hoarse, harsh above the methodical swish-and-gurgle of the river.

I hit my forehead with the palm of my hand and sucked in air two or three times, deeply.

"It's worth a try. It's worth at least a couple more casts," I said. Maybe the fish was glutting itself, in a prespawning splurge. Maybe it would come back.

With that cue ball of a skater in its jaw?

"What an idiot," I said, kicking a stone and stubbing my big toe sorely.

I got out my fly box and hunted for another big fly. Anything as long as it was big. There were no dries of any size, only a huge Marabou Muddler.

I snipped off another section of my leader, making it no longer than six and a half feet now, tapered to about twelve-pound test. No fish would break that—no fish, no matter how hard I struck.

I cast a few times and twitched the fly back across the current. The fly was not sinking and did not look like much flopping around on the surface. Perhaps the fish was deep. It might not rise again but it might—it just might—not be able to resist a big fly rolled along the bottom.

I dug into my vest and came out with a small container of split shot, three of which I extracted and pinched onto the heavy leader, just above the fly, in intervals of an inch or so. I had sworn not to fly-fish with a meat rig like this. Pure regression. But there was a huge brown in the depths of that pool. I cast sidearm, as I'd once cast night crawlers, looping the heavy lure out as far as I could without false-casting. I did not come close to reaching the heart of the pool, so I waded in, in my street shoes, above my knees. My toe stung where I'd stubbed it.

On my fifth clumsy, fruitless cast the Muddler hung up in the rocks. I jerked and pulled back with my rod, let my shoulders collapse, grabbed the line itself, and tugged until the leader broke at the highest split shot.

I was sweating now around my neck, and my legs shook, for the water was cooler than I'd thought. I could still feel the tremor in my arm. The sun had gone behind clouds; the air was brisk.

A few more casts.

Ten more casts and I'd leave off this madness. I had destroyed every idyllic touch of the day. But I kept seeing that huge boil and roll of the fish, as if a hog had been thrown, kicking, into the water. A huge fish, a monster. A once-in-a-lifetime brown.

I saw a rise along the far bank that might be a decent trout—not the big one but a good fish. I looked at the end of my leader; it was heavy enough to hoist a hippo out of the mud. I found a large Hair Coachman and managed, after four tries, to poke the leader through its eye. The nylon was so stiff that I could barely tie a simple knot. I put the leader to my mouth compulsively and tried, unsuccessfully, to chew off the stem outside the knot. Finally I left it on and began to cast rapidly, hearing the fly slap down against the rocks behind me, then slap down again on the next false cast, catch, come loose; and then I leaned into a long cast that sent the fly beyond the main current to the opposite bank. I nudged it off a rock and a fish immediately rose.

The fish had some size but I horsed it across stream roughly, rapidly, bold with my cable of a leader.

A chub. A fat, thirteen-inch chub.

Bastard!

I lifted it out summarily with my rod, which bent in a wide arc, and tried to extract the hook imbedded in the soft mouth. It wouldn't come free. I pinched the fish's head hard with the thumb and forefinger of my left hand, yanked the hook loose, and dropped the near-dead fish in the water beside me.

Two casts. Three or four more casts. No more.

When I dropped the fly into the water, to clean away the slime, it landed a foot or so from the big chub, which now floated on its side, its tail waving feebly. There may be those, who love all things great and small, who love the chub; I am not one of them. I dropped and raised the fly a few times and then, thinking it was clean, was about to raise it when I saw . . .

It couldn't be!

They did not come that big.

The fish was a yard long. It was, by a full foot, the largest brown trout I had ever seen. It was an old, hookjawed fish, eight, maybe ten pounds, and it was no more than five feet away from me. I stood paralyzed. I did not breathe.

The fish never changed its slow, even pace. It glided closer like some apparition in a Cocteau film, angled toward the chub, took the floundering fat fish in one methodical turn and swirl—crosswise in its mouth—and then, with the same slow glide, holding that fat chub as a retriever holds a shot duck, it headed back into the depths and out of sight.

I did not move for a minute. I kept watching the depths into which the fish had disappeared. Then I bit the mouthpiece off my pipe, slapped my fly sharply down on the water a dozen times, with no more than the leader beyond the tiptop. Quite hard.

I could not control my body. I was shaking maniacally. I was a mass of tics and twitches and tremors. I was totally unhinged.

Without breaking down my rod, I turned and galloped away from the river like a rhinoceros. I plunged through tangled vines and sere cattails. I tripped in a bog, nearly broke my rod, and scratched my way through a maze of long-dead raspberry bushes, back toward the car, back to the safe city.

We returned to "Eastover" to retrieve the last of our clothes and supplies. Despite the heavy rains, the ash, maple, and oak have kept most of their leaves, some of which are now orange and red. It is late September. Two bold fat raccoons came out at midday, rattled the screen doors, and rummaged around the garbage cans; they are hardly recognizable as those furry newborns I first saw in June.

I had hoped to fish the Esopus one last time, but the river was unfishable again. I had had a number of really good days there and had been dreaming of fishing below the Five Arches Bridge.

So in the evening I headed back to the reservoir, which has been such a salvation all summer. While I was stepping into my waders, a funny little man, no taller than four feet, eight inches, came up with his spinning rod and a scowl. "Last week I caught an eighteen-inch pickerel," he said.

"That's a good fish."

"Best I've taken."

I slipped the suspenders over my shoulders, straightened them, and put on my vest.

"Hooked one even bigger this afternoon. Much bigger. Maybe a foot longer he was, like so. Brought him in and knowed right away he was a bigger one'n I'd ever caught. Well, I get him and puts him on the stringer and ties the stringer to a log and keeps fishing a little ways off and when I comes back he's gone and so's the stringer."

I looked up. "You sure no one stole it?"

"Couldn't of. Didn't see no one come near it. He done

pulled it out. Biggest pickerel I ever caught. Damned shame. Never get another like him," he mumbled, "not if I fish for ten more years." And then he went off to his car.

Shades of *Jaws*. And a good omen.

Mari looked up from the Evelyn Waugh novel she was reading and wished me luck, and I headed down to the water, promising without fail to be no longer than an hour and a half. "Sure," she said, with a mock scowl.

On my first two casts I took large bluegills—fat, orange fish that raced in circles. Then I took two smallmouths, little ones that I threw back. And then a rock bass. Well, there was some action, and the light was still good. Another fifteen minutes and the big bass would start to move; I could feel it. But then the sky clouded over suddenly and a sharp wind came up—much too hard in which to cast a bug—so I breathed deeply, looked out across the long reservoir to the mauve and pale cobalt mountain ranges, and decided to fold up the season. It had been a long, interesting summer, not nearly as fertile as I would have liked, but I had brought a great portion of the lakes and bright rivers into me.

For the first time since June I unjoined my fly rod, wound in the line, and then took off the reel and slipped it into the inside pocket of my vest. "You're forty minutes early!" Mari said when I got back to the car. "Are you sick?"

"Too much wind," I said, putting my gear into the back of the battered station wagon.

"Wind? You're fished out!"

"Never!"

"Fished fully out!"

"That'll be the day."

She looked at me carefully. "If you're not sick, you're fished up to the gills. You've had all you can take for one year."

"The wind . . ."

"Bull!"

So we talked about it, laughing, on the short drive back to "Eastover" and made a large bright fire in the fireplace, and in front of the fire, while she finished her Waugh, I clipped the flies out of the lamb's-wool patch on my vest, slipped my reels into their chamois bags, took down two other fly rods and slipped them into their cases, and packed everything into a carryall. I thought of Thoreau's "I love best to have each thing in its season only, and enjoy doing without it at all other times."

Then, for some unaccountable reason, I began to think of Montana.

Part Two

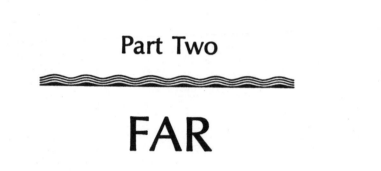

FAR

4
Westward

I love the wild not less than the good. The wildness and adventure that are in fishing still recommend it to me.

HENRY DAVID THOREAU

ON the day before I last flew west, for a long-awaited week of fishing in September, I witnessed this event on my upper Broadway.

First, according to what I saw, a cab driver leaned out of his window and hollered at a double-parked sky-blue Cadillac that was blocking his way. Then a long-haired kid—lean, with pinched cheeks, about twenty—put a bony hand out of the Cadillac's left window, with the middle finger extended and jiggling up and down.

"Get the hell out of the way," the cabbie yelled, "you lousy bastard!"

This time the lean young man decided that no mother could talk to him like that, leaped out of his car, and strode boldly toward the cab. In his right hand he held a baseball bat. As I watched, quite disembodied, with no urge or reflex to move, the boy reached the cab, lifted the bat, and began an incessant battering of the top of the trunk. Again and again he lifted the bat and smashed it down with all his power.

A group of onlookers quickly assembled. Several took out cameras. No one said a word. They, like the great movie heroes of the West, let a man play his own hand out. So, apparently, did I.

A moment later I heard the cab driver shout, "Is he hitting my cab? Is that what the bastard's doing? Is that *my* cab he's hitting?"

There seemed no question of this to me; it could not have been otherwise.

In a moment the man was out of his cab, and at the same time—freed by a latch on his dashboard—the trunk door swung up. He raced toward it. The young man loped back to his Cadillac, laughing wildly, and locked himself in. The cameras clicked, the onlookers kept gathering.

In the trunk of the cab I saw one object: a gigantic hammer, the largest hammer I'd ever seen. Its handle was the length of a tennis racket. It was not a mallet or an axe but a hammer. Why would anyone buy such a tool? What was its use? Why would one leave it, alone, neatly placed in the center of a trunk that flipped open with the flick of a switch? The cabbie grabbed the hammer on the run and headed toward the Cadillac. He was yelling, over and over, "Hit my cab, will you? Hit my cab, will you?"

What now? I wondered. Surely the man won't hit the car with *that!*

"Hit my cab, will you? Hit my cab, will you?" He was brandishing the hammer, waving it back and forth like a weapon of early war.

He'll merely threaten, I thought. No one would wield a thing like that with serious intent.

The crowd had increased considerably by now; people lined both sides of the street. They were back just far enough to enable the hand to be played out. Some were cheering. They were having a perfectly marvelous time.

The cabbie got to the front left window—behind which I could see the lean boy laughing wildly—and abruptly swung the hammer at it with full force, fracturing the glass. One second it was whole; the next, a mosaic of tiny irregular rectangles radiated from a center hole. "Hit my cab, will you?" he shouted and fractured the front window just as the boy leaped out the door on the passenger's side and high-stepped across the street, his face sober now, yelling, "What are you doing? What the fuck are you doing, man?"

"Hit my cab, will you? Hit my cab, will you?" The cabbie began to batter the hood of the Cadillac, denting it sharply. He would swing and there would be a strange loud sound and then I would see the dent. The crowd cheered. The boy was across the street, waving his arms, shouting; I could not hear what he said. Without turning to the crowd, the cabbie methodically smashed both headlights.

I turned then and headed home. I wanted all my affairs in order before I went west.

On the plane, the odd sight of the soundless movie, a situational comedy, the characters a middle-aged man, balding—his gestures vulgar, inane—and several truly handsome women, quite slim and bright-eyed. What would one say to such women? They were chic, animated mannequins, very pretty, very pert; they spoke with great fluidity but, since I could not hear their voices, I did not know what they were saying. They laughed and chatted, but it did not seem that what they said could matter very much. I thought of other talk I could not understand, either, and what lay behind the talk: ingenious academic chatter that threatened always to destroy the simple but deep love I had for teaching, gibberish art talk in the magazines, the nagging and superior talk of the critics who, in some cosmic Mah-Jongg game, played for reputations.

I was headed for Montana and I did not want to think of such talk; I did not want to think of all the things I hated and that were unreal. I had Hemingway, Big Old Daddy Ernie, at my shoulder, and the B.O.D.E. told me that the world would slip away from me if I worried too much about all that; and I was going to Montana, where I had always wanted to go in the fall, and I thought of how the rivers would be low and cold and how the big brown trout would come lunging up for one of my flies. Only suddenly, bursting in on me, would be some city image, like that cab driver pounding the Cadillac with his hammer or one of those prissy colleagues of mine at the university who laughed only at literary jokes, told me my fish writing would destroy my academic career, and could not say four words without uttering a *mise-en-scène* or a *raison d'être*. We were hooked up to so many wires: we were wired to our past and to the drug of the media and to the itch—oh, it was always there—to get on and make it and prove who we were and play not in our own game with our own rules but in the world's game.

Suddenly a fellow passenger, hooked to the screen by more than eye, earphones inserted in his ears like a doctor's stethoscope, rocketed with laughter, as if electrified by some mysterious inner coil.

In "The Disasters of War" Goya shows an unusual view of man: men are sliced from the groin up or hung from a tree and pulled down; one, without arms, is impaled upon a sharpened stump; then there are the arms without the man and the torso without anything else. Goya asks, "And this, too?"

That, too. I have not seen war and do not want to, though it exists now as then. But I have seen a mere arm, a mere leg, a disembodied brain—oh, many of those in academe—and other disasters too numerous to mention. They are everywhere. I did not want to escape from them, but right then I did not want my mind to toss them at me; I was on a plane, high over the Midwest, suspended in time, traveling in a modern machine to Montana by myself, and I wanted to think of what would be and of the other times I had been to the West. At first the images were scattered, fragmentary, blurred, but I took out a pad and began to write them out, slowly at first, then with my hand racing across the page until I had to slow it down, make each letter more deliberate.

As I was writing, I remembered about how it was in the Army when I first began to write: how I would carry two paperback books in the top pockets of my field jacket and find time, somehow, to read both of them each day. I had wanted to write, but other things had kept me from trying when I was a kid; then I was past twenty and I still had not begun to read seriously or to write. I had felt myself slipping into other worlds, where I did not want to spend my life, and thought I was too late and began to read like a madman, two, three books a day some days, grasping at words, reading so fast the plots blurred and even the titles faded and disappeared. But I had this desperate feeling then that I would be one of the disasters of the ever-continuing war if I did not work harder, burn away the dross, shape and target the design of my brain.

I would rent a typewriter at the Enlisted Men's Club, a machine hooked to a clock, and sit in front of it while the seconds ticked away and finally I would pound and hack obscenities onto the blank white sheet, rip the paper out, ball it up tighter than an ice ball, insert another dime, and start again. There was no hope for it.

Later, when I was living alone in Greenwich Village, in a furnished room with puke-green walls the size of a john or a tomb, I tried even harder, and, like the Chinese two-finger puzzle, the harder I tried the worse my prose grew. I had taken several roads at once after that, into the academic world and into the business world, because I had many expenses, but always I had kept that flame alive. I was very busy for many years, working at two jobs, then a third, concurrently, for when the flame grew and I could control it I used it for other purposes—writing other people's books for them, writing books on assignment, writing literary criticism. I was "some twentie sev'ral men each sev'ral houre." I justified these things to myself by saying that I needed the money, which I did; that I was learning my craft, quite late and under raw necessity, which I was; and that Balzac and others had done the same thing, which they had.

So I never felt corrupted or destroyed by this other writing, but after a few years of it I decided I ought to have my name on everything I wrote and then I decided to write only what I wanted to write, my way. Mostly, now, I wrote about rivers and fishing. That seemed a small canvas, but it was always green and flowing and there was not one but always dozens of different stories to write, and some of them seemed to me very moving (though someone called one of them "mush" and misquoted me to prove his point), and some seemed very funny. If it was a small canvas, as it probably was, it was not only what I knew best and in the best way but what I wanted to write. "Paint your stovepipe," said Cézanne. The critical articles, which had been published in "important" literary quarterlies and which had won me promotions at the university, were without color: they had no rivers or trees or live things in them. They did not allow me to be "cousin to the pine and the rock."

So I was going to Montana to catch some fish and perhaps write some stories with rivers and trees and fish in them, and perhaps more, and older stories kept pouring from my brain as I sat back in my seat and looked out over the vast fields of cloud from a plane that seemed not to be moving.

I thought of that first time, when I had been an Eastern innocent out West. "The lake for big ones," Sandy Bing had written to me from Croix Chapeau, France, twenty years ago. I had been discharged from the Army several months earlier, and when I wrote him that I was bent on driving across country, he had sent me a concise letter listing a dozen or so good waters. I had driven out alone, exploring here and there, picking cherries in Colorado, washing dishes in Wyoming, and when I circled back, not yet having fished, I sought out his lake "for big ones." The lake was on the Continental Divide, surrounded by dreary sagebrush flats, and I had caught huge trout on a Wob-l-rite from the shore, in the springs. I had taken an enormous number of big trout on my spinning rod—trout to make the eyes of an Easterner weened on hatchery fish bulge.

When I drove out again, five years ago, I planned to stay at that lake again. I thought that my son Paul might take his first really big fish there. Hadn't Dave Whitlock told me of a whalish trout he'd hooked on a fly in that lake, that had actually *towed* his canoe for twenty minutes?

By then I had long since lost my heart to the fly rod. I had grown to love rivers—and my plans featured the Madison,

the Firehole, Henrys Fork of the Snake, perhaps the Big
Hole, hopefully Armstrong Spring Creek, probably the
Yellowstone. Nelson Spring Creek? Rock Creek? The Beaverhead? I had lived with those names all that winter, for a
half-dozen city winters. I had lived with the huge trout I had
seen in Dan Bailey's and Bud Lilly's catalogs. I felt, as I
drove west that time, like a little boy heading into a candy
shop, where he'd be surrounded by innumerable bins of
sweets, where he'd be unable to dispose calmly of his well-
earned nine cents.

I dreamed of the rivers, but it did not work out that way.

On our third day, fishing a long brown Leech on a Hi-D
line, I hooked something that went steadily, merrily on its
way, that stripped line to the backing without so much as a
nervous wiggle or rush, that then wound my four-pound-test
leader summarily around some weeds and swam off, no
doubt chuckling mightily at this Eastern dude. And I was
hooked. Except for three short forays onto the rivers, I never
left the lake that trip.

"You'll get unbelievable cutthroats and brooks," Bud Lilly
told me at his Trout Shop in West Yellowstone, "once you
learn the house rules." I had gone out that first night, an
hour after we arrived from the grueling four-day car trip, not
knowing one of the house rules, and I had fished three hours
without a tap. I had never fly-fished a lake for trout before,
and as I looked out over the huge expanse of this slate-gray
lake I did not know where to cast, how deep to fish my fly,
what time of the day to fish, what fly to use, how to retrieve.
I thought of what I'd learned on the Beaverkill and the Battenkill and the Willowemoc and shrugged my shoulders.

Others caught fish that night. But they were casting a full
forty feet farther than I could. What flies were they using?
Was everything I had learned in the East—from casting to fly
imitation—useless?

I had an eight-and-a-half-foot glass rod, a sinking No. 8 line, and a four-pound-test leader. The leader had seemed adequate at first, but when I caught nothing I thought of going finer. Was that why others caught fish? I knew nothing about the proper flies for the lake and bought a dozen weird wooly-worm patterns, from bright chartreuse to black, from the tackle shop at the lodge. I would not have used them for sunfish back East, but I had seen local patterns work too often to think of trying my delicate Eastern flies.

My luck changed when I met Thom Green. He hailed me from the porch of his cabin, which was next to ours, and soon gave me three flies. They were long brown wooly-worm patterns with brown marabou tails. The Leech. That's what the fish were on. How would I have known? I used nothing else in the lake for ten days. One of the flies took eleven fish and is now a ragged memento, its leaded body bare, of the trip. I lost the other two in fish and Thom replaced them with three others, fresh from the vise he had set up on his dining-room table.

I watched Thom carefully that night. He was tall, solid, nearly bald and consistently amazed me by throwing out well over 100 feet of line. I did not realize until later that he and most of the other fly-fishers were using a shooting head, which I had never seen before. He would cast and then he would wait, and *wait*, and then he would finally retrieve with studied slowness. I had not waited, and I had been retrieving far too fast. I changed to a Hi-D line and fished deep and slow and with slow twitches, pointing my rod toward the water as Thom did. He also told me that an important part of this fishing was *position*. There was a channel in this lake, headed by a major spring—the one that I had fished from shore many years earlier, now properly closed to fishing. There were deep holes here and there, if you knew where to find them. When the weeds came up in early July and the water warmed, the fish schooled in the channel and headed toward the springs. You had to position your boat just right to fish the channel properly; there was a pole and a chimney which, if properly aligned, told you you were in the right spot. And in the early morning, before the sun broke over the mountains, there was one man, an old "regular," who could find his way in the dark; other boats waited for him in the cold darkness, then used him as a point man and found the hole and channel after he had anchored.

I began to catch fish sporadically. I fished for two or three hours, slowly, steadily, without a strike—and then took three fish one after the other. These were big fish by Eastern standards: two- and three-pound cutthroats and brooks. I would be plying the dull art of the slow retrieve and suddenly the rod would thump down. My four-pound-test leader held, and I did not think to change it. Paul caught two fine brookies, and Mari caught a couple of landscapes.

Soon I would head off for the rivers.

But then I lost the big one that summarily took me into the weeds. There was something about its nonchalant power, its sense of total authority. It was that indifferent heavy tug, the challenge of being totally out of control that stung my blood.

The next morning I was out at four o'clock and fished until past noon; I fished from seven that evening until well after dark. Oh, yes, I caught fish now and then: at noon, at nine at night. You never knew when they would strike, when a big one would take, but you knew they were there, fish big enough to set your heart thumping.

I saw a seven-pounder come from the lake. There were reports that a six-pound brook trout had been taken the week before we arrived. At dinner I faced the awesome armada of mounted trout on the walls of the lodge—four, five, six of them, all well over ten pounds, all taken on flies. In my dreams I faced those huge trout. And in the morning, as I eased my boat into the spring, I could look down and see six- and eight-pound brooks and cutthroats swimming leisurely, safely, in the protected water. Each day there were more of them; the migration to the cold springs had begun. I desperately wanted to take at least one of the monsters.

Bud Lilly understood. My wife could not. I had come for a much-needed rest, she advised me, not for this insane ritual of waking at four o'clock and coming off the water only to collapse for a few hours and then fish again until dark.

Thom, an Oklahoman who could and did fish the area regularly, loved the lake too, but he thought I ought to sample the rivers, and we went off several days together. Bud Lilly pointed out a few good spots on the Madison to us, using the famous "Fish Map" on the wall of his shop. I asked him which flies I would need, and he suggested the Rio Grande King, which is a fine all-purpose Western fly, and an indelicate concoction called, appropriately, the Bitch Creek Special. It did not look like a Red Quill. It reminded me immediately of a tarantula I had once seen, with its big dark body and rubber legs. It was not precisely the fly I'd have chosen for dusk fishing on the Battenkill.

I fished behind Thom on the big Madison. Bud's last words as we left had been ironic but firm: "Don't drown." When I first saw that huge river, with its bed of greased bowling balls, I knew what he meant; I stayed close to the brush along the banks. I fished dry, with a huge Sofa Pillow first and then the Rio Grande King. The wind buffaloed down the river, wrecking my casts; the buffaloing river quickly wrecked the float when I did get my fly on the water. I got hung up in the bushes; I watched those big flies slingshot out and drop like rocks on the churning water; I could not control my float. I caught nothing. Above me, Thom caught eight or ten rainbows, some up to sixteen inches.

I scurried up the rock embankment and walked upstream to watch him. He was just releasing another fine rainbow.

"Fine fishing," he called.

"Haven't gotten a thing."

"Fishing wet?"

"Dry."

"Try that Bitch Creek or a big black nymph," he said. "Fish it across and down, on a long line, like you do for steelhead."

"Never fished for steelhead."

"Well, on a long line. You know."

I opened my fly box, got out one of the big flies I had bought from Bud, looked at it, and shuddered. On my first cast, as the fly turned and paused at the end of its downstream sweep, there was a sudden sharp tug—and then the fly was gone.

"Fish?" called Thom.

"Broke him off."

I tied on the second and last Bitch Creek Special and a minute later snapped it off, too.

Thom came up and looked at my leader. "For the Beaverkill, maybe, but not here. Remind me to give you one of mine when we get back to the lake. Meanwhile, break it off about here."

That left a stout seven feet, with a point of about eight- to ten-pound test.

Thom gave me a big black Whitlock Nymph, and a few casts later I had caught and released my first Madison rainbow, a fine fifteen-incher.

Back at the lake that night I took four good cutthroats, and then several more the following morning. The lake was continuing to grow on me. The long casts, the slow methodical retrieves, the expectation each time of a really big fish hypnotized me. I could not get enough of it. I was out each morning at four o'clock, taking my spot in the ridiculous armada behind the point man; I did not want to come in for lunch, and I did not want to come in at night—even when the winds sweeping through the valley raked the waters to sealike froth.

Several days later, Thom insisted I had to try the middle Madison, above Quake Lake, and the Firehole in Yellowstone Park. On the way, we saw four fishermen on the bank of a small feeder creek, with more than ten trout each, the fish neatly laid out in rows on the bank. I told Thom I remembered the days when I had taken a limit whenever I could but that I had stopped when I saw the Eastern rivers decimated by such pressure.

"There are a lot of fish out here," he said, "but the West will go the same way if it's not cared for. Those guys you saw are a vanishing species. There are more out here—where the ethic still includes taking what it's your *right* to take—but it's changing."

Mari was with us, and Thom promised to find her a spot along the Firehole where she would not be molested by bears or tourists; my wife paints better when there are no bears or tourists. She waited in the car patiently while we fished a pleasant section of the middle Madison, and then Thom drove us along a back road in the park and finally stopped off to the side, above a meadow that sloped down to the Firehole. The big Madison had been awesome, even frightening; the middle Madison was more manageable, and I took two decent browns on a small Sofa Pillow.

I had heard a great deal about the Firehole and was anxious to try it. I helped Mari set up her easel, satisfied her that there were no other cars in the area and that none would come back this far from the main roads. Then Thom and I headed down the hill.

What a haunting river the Firehole is! Immaculately clear, sweeping glides, smoke from hot springs rising here and there along the banks, the water crystalline and quick. Though it was the worst of days to fish it—the clouds lowering, a stiff upstream wind—you could feel you were in the presence of something majestic, rare.

The section Thom had brought me to was obviously not heavily fished, and as far as we could see, upstream and down, there was not another fisherman. When we got to the bank, he told me to look carefully before casting. I did so. There was some slack water on our side, then a brisk center current; along the opposite meadow bank there were several yards of slower, eddying water. I saw a flash in the center current; then a fish tailed. I nudged Thom, pointed, and began to ready my rod.

"That's nothing," he said. "Small fish. Don't bother with them."

I looked again. Several more fish broke surface. I wanted to go after them.

"There," said Thom, pointing.

"Where?"

"Along the far bank. Right next to it. They're working. I was worried the wind and the oncoming rain would put them down."

I searched the slower water between the center current and the opposite bank carefully. Nothing. I could not see a fish moving.

"Guess they've stopped," I said.

"Nonsense!"

I've always been proud of my fish sight, but this time I did

not see a thing—not a rise form, not a flash, not a whisk of a
tail.

"Look," said Thom, beckoning to me to follow the line of
his arm. "There, below that clump of high grass. No more
than two, three inches from the bank."

"Bubbles?"

"That's a big fish. And there's another just below—and
there, two more. They're all big."

"You're putting me on. Those are bubbles. I may be an
Eastern innocent but I know the difference between a sipping
rise and bubbles."

"Watch," he said. He stripped line, false-cast backhand a
few times—to protect himself from the sharp upstream
wind—and then, shaking his rod to "S" the belly of his cast,
laid the line down delicately a foot or two above the bubbles
we had seen. The center current straightened the curves, the
little nymph floated a foot or two downstream, and then
Thom raised his rod quickly. The rod bent and the line tightened. A second later a beautiful brown of more than two
pounds leaped twice, went into the center current, stripped a
dozen yards of line, and slipped free of the hook.

The fish had been on for no more than a minute, but I
was convinced. Did Thom really have to say, as he did while
reeling in, "Bubbles?"

I had trouble trying to cast backhanded in the stiff wind
but managed to take two small browns in the current on casts
that never reached the far bank. Then the rains came and we
rushed up the hill and found Mari in the car, muttering
about how the tourists had flocked by, looking at the "real
live artist" as if she were a bear. I had seen her madder, but I
had never seen a better landscape of hers than the one in the
back of the station wagon.

As we headed back to the lake in the heavy rain, Thom

said, "Fishing these rivers is like playing the various instruments of an orchestra. The Firehole is like playing a violin; it requires a delicate touch, expensive instruments, and great attention to detail."

"I can't argue with that," I muttered, thinking of bubbles.

"A stream like the upper or middle Madison is more like playing the horn. It requires excellent technique but not the finesse of the violin. Now and then you can blow a blurp and survive it." He paused for a moment. "The lower Madison is like playing a percussion instrument. You use big flies, heavy leaders—*heavy leaders*, Nick!—and long, relatively clumsy casts. It's like beating a bass drum."

I was fascinated by these Western rivers and wanted to return to them. But the next morning put an end to all thoughts of leaving the lake. Slowly retrieving one of Thom's Leeches about ten o'clock that morning, I hooked onto another railroad train.

There was a sudden tightening of the line and then the same methodical movement away from the boat. I held the rod high, played the line out by hand until all the stripping coils were gone, and then listened as the reel unwound slowly. The fish was in no hurry. I tried to turn it. I put pressure on the line, but there was not a wiggle or a turn. I could not stop or deter or even slow down the fish. I knew it would get into the weeds in a few moments, so I held the rod in my left hand, hauled anchor with my right, and then stood astounded while the boat eased its way after the taut line. The fish—though Paul to this day calls me a fantasist—was pulling my boat!

In another few minutes it was all over.

My heart beat heavily, my forehead throbbed. I could tell the line was still hooked onto something, but there was no movement. I rowed to the spot, looked down, and saw that the line was wound five or six times around a clump of weeds. There was no fly and no fish.

"In open water you might handle one of those big ones on a light tippet," said Thom as, shakily, I told him what had happened. "But not in this lake; not in the summer, when the weeds are high. Why didn't you remind me to give you one of my leaders?"

For our last four days, I fished with one of Thom's leaders. He's a mathematician and had worked out a formula that assured even a duffer like me a decent turnover with those heavy flies. The tippet tested about ten pounds; Thom said he sometimes went to twelve pounds in this lake. I caught a spate of three- and four-pounders which did not seem shy of a leader the diameter of a clothesline. At various times I tried a Sculpin fly, a large Marabou Muddler, shrimp flies, damselfly nymphs, even a snail imitation; all, Thom said, had their moments. This week did not contain one of them. The Leech prevailed and did all my business.

I had learned what Bud Lilly called the "house rules," and by the end of our stay I was ready to cast off all further worldly responsibilities and resign myself to living at the lake forever, lulled by the long casts and slow retrieves and shocked into unforgetfulness by the big fish. I loved the violins and horns and bass drums I had heard, if all too briefly; some day I would come back to play them again. But I had gotten hooked on this lake, this still and slate-gray water, and my winter dreams—despite all my plans—would be of it and of the slow, thumping power of its huge fish.

I remembered, too, high over the Dakotas, the next year, when we had gone west again, and a particular moment, sitting beneath Varney's Bridge. Then I was there, cleaning my two fish again in the shadows, watching the Madison, still strong in spring flood.

I had finished plying whatever fly-fishing art and skill I could bring to the river. A deep slow ache, not uncomfortable, had worked its way into my shoulders; the back of my right hand, from the wrist to beyond the knuckles, was red, somewhat distended, and stinging from the sun. I had cast many times that afternoon.

It had been a good afternoon on a hard, turbulent river. Some giant stone flies, larger than grasshoppers and called salmon flies here, fluttered heavily off the swollen water. Now and then a sharp spurt flew up from the rapids, and I knew a rainbow or brown had taken one of the fallen flies or perhaps a high-floating nymph, of which I had seen many.

The point of the hatch was ten miles upstream. I had seen rubber rafts finish their float and lean, rough-spoken men pile out with boat nets full of fat trout—two- and three- and even four-pounders that curled in the bottom meshes of the huge nets like gigantic worms in a can. Those men had been fishing with spinning rods, with live stone flies impaled on a bait hook below a red-and-white bobber. They were then going to stash their fish in a portable icebox and make another run down the stretch of river that passed the point of the hatch. Even so fecund a river as the Madison could not bear such slaughter.

There were dozens of other boats on the river up there— more rubber rafts, johnboats, canoes, McKenzie River boats—and thirty or forty fishermen, scrambling along the banks, asking everyone else, "Where is it?" I had very much wanted to see the point of a great stone-fly hatch myself just once—with every trout moving, ecstatic, caught in that "sensual music," vulnerable; but I did not want to be a part of such a circus.

So I drove down to Varney's Bridge and fished far downriver and caught fewer and smaller fish, my way, by myself. A half dozen or so had either come up for the Sofa Pillow or taken my orange Whitlock Nymph. They were not trophies but solid fish and had fought hard in the fast, relentless current of the Madison. I had caught five and kept the two smallest, bright silver fourteen-inchers that would make a good breakfast. The river, during the stone-fly hatch, could afford me the luxury of two fourteen-inchers.

As I slit the trout, made two cuts below the gills and prepared to gut and run them clean, two or three giant stone flies rose and fluttered wildly; then one fell back, whirling on the churning surface and racehorsing downstream with the current. I followed it with my eyes, squinting against the bright sheen of the sun on the fast, broken water to where it bobbed and turned, fluttering, then lying still. A sudden splash—and it is taken.

Then the swallows, fork-tailed and fleet, begin to dip and dart and disappear beneath the bridge and reappear. I try to follow one but cannot. I strain, but as hard as my eyes try, until they blur, the birds deftly interweave in aerial ballet, cross and vanish beneath the bridge and then appear again, and I cannot tell one from the other. They are identical shuttles, moving at phenomenal speed. Only if I watch closely can I see them balance vertically in the air, poised, open their thin bills, and nab a salmon fly in flight. Behind the sky tapestry, there is bird and death, the fleet hunt and blood. It is not a game.

Then tannish caddis flies begin to hatch, softer, smaller, whirling: clouds of them. From where I crouch beneath the bridge a brief patch of the vast magical Montana sky has gone mad. Dipping and darting, gliding with faultless grace, the black shuttles weave the sky with master strokes, their shadows waking the stream further—making all alive—where now the steady spurt-splash of feeding fish has begun. I see a heavy-bodied brown roll in the current above me, making a lathed arc. I see with the eye of a man who has lived too long in cities, and with the fisherman's eye, a corrective lens, healing.

Other fishermen have come to the bridge now. I hear one of them shout above me, another upstream. The spur of excitement goads them. I envision their eyes wide and intense. I hear them catch the whir of the birds, the frenzied slash of big trout in hard current, in their voices.

But I sit hushed and quiet in the shadows beneath Varney's Bridge, finishing the last of my preparations, holding the fish by their empty jaws and shaking them lightly in the current, allowing the current to find the contours of their bodies, to clean them of bits of grass, twigs, and blood. For a moment they seem alive: wet and lithe and able to swim off.

I look again at the clouds of tan caddis, the whirling birds, the bright river that has come fully alive. My eyes freshen with wonder. . . .

And then, the two trout in my canvas bag, I stood and left the shadows of the bridge. I remember the weight of the trout in the creel slung lightly over my shoulder—but they were the least I took from the Madison that day.

Paul caught his first trout on a fly that trip. Thinking of that, I began to think also of how fly-fishing differs from all other forms of fishing and how desperate fathers become, sometimes, to share their deepest pleasures with sons. I had already heard of innumerable cases of children who had been given vigorous, tenacious, and even expensive training in a sport only to despise it for the rest of their lives. I suppose we like what we like not out of obligation, ever, or because we would *like* to like it, but because something in us responds as naturally as a trout to a mayfly to something in the action. It cannot be forced. Particularly not fly-fishing, which is a rather demanding affair.

Still, we dream. Paul *seemed* to have a genuine liking for fishing, especially when he caught some fish, which he often did. He had natural coordination and a good eye and became an excellent spin-fisherman by the age of nine or ten.

"Why didn't you start him with a fly rod?" asked several fly-fishing friends.

A good question. I was already deeply hooked on the fly rod by then, and I wanted to share with Paul fly names, hatches, rises, leaders, and all the other arcane details that so absorb and delight the lover of fly-fishing. I told them that I had not started with a fly rod and that I wanted him to catch fish.

"Did you always have to catch fish?"

"No."

"Anyway," one said, "he'll catch plenty, soon enough, because the fly rod, properly used, will catch as many trout as bait or spinners." I had to agree.

I had rather slowly worked my way toward the fly rod over a good many years, I told them. No one I knew fly-fished, and it seemed an impossibly complicated way to catch trout—if indeed you could catch them that way. I wasn't convinced, not until the day I watched a man take four, on a dry fly; each time a fish rose, I felt a sharp twinge, like an electric shock, in my chest.

Robert Frost, when asked why he still wrote with a defined meter and often in rhyme, replied that it was no fun to play tennis without a net. Part of the pleasure we take in any sport depends upon the reasonable limits we set to our freedom: the slalom skier must move between certain carefully positioned upright poles, the baseball player within foul lines. The basketball hoop is neither too small nor too large, but as basketball players grew taller, rules were added to maintain a fair chance—the three-second rule, goal tending. This denied to the merely big man an unwarranted advantage by prohibiting him from camping under the basket or stopping the offensive shot when it was on its downward course. Rules enhance the quality and pleasure of a game, never diminish them. It is not sporting or even reasonable to play basketball with a ball so large it will scarcely fit through a hoop, or with one hand tied behind one's back. This becomes affectation, fiddling around.

The object of all fishing is to gull a fish. Some anglers find pleasure in doing this by any legal means; I like a prescribed court, a code of reasonable limits. My object, by choice, is to gull the fish with a single fly. I would use a ten-pound leader if that would fool it; it usually won't. Smaller rods do not increase my pleasure, nor are they necessarily sportier—since you may tire a fish and even kill it in the longer fight required, and most casting situations demand a longer rod. Dry flies are more pleasurable than wet flies, at least for me, because you can see the fish rise to them. But often only sinking flies will move the bigger fish, or any fish, or even reach any of them. Some attempt at imitation of the natural insect on which trout are feeding brings me more satisfaction than merely luring them to an attractor pattern, because you have had to live more deeply in the trout's domain, solve the riddle of its selective feeding. Ultimately, I do not fish for the trout's pleasure or convenience but for mine. I do not think the fish has a sense of fairness—or a sense of very much at all.

On that trip Paul had caught a fat cutthroat in the Shoshone, as we approached Yellowstone Park, and several good fish in Henrys Lake—on his spinning rod. He had confidence in it. He was unwilling to give it up. He had traveled two thousand miles and he wanted to catch trout—which meant, for him, the spinning rod.

I had traveled two thousand miles, too, and I wanted to enjoy myself, not worry whether or not my son became a flyfisherman. So we both fished the lake and I enjoyed myself royally—as I always do when I fish—and Paul got good and properly bored and began to go mountain climbing.

On our last day I arranged to take my first float trip down the Madison with Mike Lilly, Bud's son. He asked if I would be going alone, and I said I wasn't sure. Then at the last minute Paul decided to forego mountain climbing and come along, though he only brought his spinning rod. I took two fly rods.

In the morning I raised a few fish but each time struck late; we were floating too fast for a second cast. Then I took a few small fish and Paul took a small rainbow on a spinner. I could see that he did not want to use a fly rod in the boat.

We had a pleasant lunch in the grass above a fast run and then walked to where a channel entered the main river. The smaller water immediately appealed to me; with its bends and pools and gentler speed it reminded me of Eastern rivers I loved. We came to one run where a narrow, brisk current widened into a pool about fifteen feet across. I asked Paul to try it first, perhaps with a fly, but he preferred to use his trusty spinner. He cast upstream and retrieved the lure with short deft twitches. A trout struck and then was off. On the next cast he pricked another. The run was filled with good fish.

"Try a fly," I suggested.

"I didn't bring a fly rod."

"I brought an extra," I reminded him.

"Well . . ." He looked at Mike. "That's all right. I'll try the spinner again, if you don't mind."

Mike told me of a pool around the bend, where the conservation department had shocked up several four-pounders, and said he'd stay with Paul and show him another spot or two among the channels.

I did not catch one of the big ones, but I did take a good seventeen-inch brown and several smaller ones on a Whitlock Hopper. It was fine, careful fishing, and I enjoyed being able to wade—and being off by myself. My code did not have to be Paul's code. One came to rivers to pleasure oneself, not please one's father's whims.

When I came back around the bend an hour later, I saw Paul, knee-deep in the first run and fast to a good trout. He was smiling broadly and Mike was coaching him in a quiet voice.

Paul was using a fly rod.

I came up close to Mike and asked if this was Paul's first trout. Yes, it was his first trout on a fly—and he was radiant.

"He came right up, Dad," the boy said, scarcely willing to turn his head away from the splashing fish. "Mike said they'd be up next to that rock, where the current slaps against it, and they were. And one came right up and sucked it down. And I struck just right—"

"He struck it perfectly," said Mike.

"And he was on."

"And there he is!" I said as the fish jumped, a brightly colored fourteen-inch brown. Paul netted the fish himself, on the third swing, and then raised it high, that huge smile still plastered all over his face.

And in the darkened car, riding at dusk back to our cabin after Mike had left us, Paul chattered on in luxuriant detail about the other two fish he later caught that afternoon on a dry fly. He also told me about a good one Mike had caught under an alder, while he looked on from the bank not ten feet from where the trout rose.

"I saw it all," he said with animation. "He cast perfectly. Just five feet above the tree. And he snaked the line a little— you know, to give it a good drift . . ."

"I know."

"And the fly floated perfectly. He's a terrific fisherman, and a terrific guy; he told me to crouch right there above the tree, so I could see it all. He said there *had* to be a fish there. He'd changed his leader tippet and put on a little gray caddis imitation—because he'd seen some caddis, of course. . . ."

"Of course."

"And he only false-cast once and then laid the fly down perfectly. The water was just like a piece of liquid crystal. I could see everything. I think my heart stopped as that fly floated down toward the tree, then under it, and then the trout came from nowhere—from under the bank, I think. It was the fastest thing I've ever seen. The water was so clear I could see everything that happened—and, wow, that was the most beautiful thing I've ever seen. I felt this strange shot of electricity go through me when I saw it come up suddenly, from nowhere, and turn, and take the fly. The most beautiful thing. . . ."

"I know," I said quietly.

We watched the last purple and pink of a Montana sunset fade below some shadowy mountains far off to the right.

"Like electricity. *Wham!*" He slammed a fist into his palm. "*Wham!* Just like that."

"I know."

I dreamed of other voyages I knew: those of Odysseus and Pound's seafarer, Hölderlin to Patmos and Yeats to his Byzantium, Ahab in his mad pursuit and Whitman's passage to "more than India," and Keats—"on the viewless wings of poesy"—with his nightingale, voyages near and far and inward to places holy and dangerous and rare . . . and then the plane angled, swooped like a great bird, and touched down at the airstrip in a place called Butte.

5

River Touring

Eventually, all things merge into one, and a river runs through it. . . . I am haunted by waters.

NORMAN MACLEAN

I

SUDDENLY you're gliding. The rubber raft comes clear of the shore gravel, swivels, picks up the main current, and the guide's oars grow rhythmic, then faint in your ears. Sitting in the front seat, with only inches between you and the water, you look out over the winding expanse of river before you, up at the yellowed cottonwoods and pink and yellow aspens, at the slope of the hills and at the stark gray buttes, up toward higher peaks—with jagged patches of snow at their crests. The air is crisp. The vast sky is pale cobalt, almost cloudless.

You strip line from your reel, test the knot on your fly.

You look backward and a ruddy face nods, so you turn front again and begin to watch the ever-varying line where the moving river meets the shore. Sky and hills disappear. You feel the raft slip into faster current. The willows, where they border and droop into the river, are moving upstream. Motion. All is changing now. You pass a pinched bend and watch the lace of the current dance and widen; you watch the eddies behind a dozen rocks, the slower water beneath overhanging willows, slight changes in the conformation of the shoreline that create a constant series of small, moving targets, each different, each racing upstream as you float, never stopping.

Targets, one after the other now: pinched pockets, patches of backwater spotted with foam, swirls. Targets. Every one of them slipping noiselessly upstream, back, past you and out of range.

You begin to cast. There is time for one shot, maybe two if you're lightning fast, a third before the target is gone. Inches are critical. Too far out and by now you know there will be nothing. You must watch the current: with fast water between you and the shore you must curve-cast properly, put the fly downstream of the line. Every muscle and nerve of your body is awake. Your eyes cannot turn for a second. You do not want to miss one likely spot. There! And there! That run behind the boulder. Under the tree. In the slack water right up against the shore. Again. Then into the pocket where the mudbank goes concave. Pick that pocket. Into the foam line. Into that two-foot eddy behind the boulder. It is like jump shooting, but faster—extraordinarily fast. The targets never stop.

Then down a quick sluice, a moment's rest, quick glances to both riverbanks now. Left or right?

"There!" Phil says, his voice a sharp invitation, and I cast backhand to the right bank, into that pocket. "Again," and the fly is up and, without a false cast, upstream and into the same pocket. "And again!" I strain, accelerate, and force the fly upstream farther this time. It lands within inches of the bank, pauses, then begins to shoot downstream as I strip line frantically. A good brown rolls, lunges, misses. I feel it in my chest. I breathe out sharply and turn to Phil. He nods; yes, he saw. I start to reel in. "Left side. Left. Quick!" he says, and I look and see the pocket and put line in the air again. My wrist already aches, my casting hand is calloused. A deep, dull, but satisfying pain is beginning to work into my shoulders.

We are floating the Big Hole below Divide, Montana. We have floated the river three times this week, and slowly I have been learning the mechanics of this new thing for me—float fishing—feeling the full challenge of it grow, and earning some of its special rewards. Later this week we may try the Beaverhead, then perhaps the Jefferson or Madison, whichever is fishing better.

Phil Wright has recently developed these Fall River Tours. From his home base in Wise River, Phil is equipped to provide excellent lodging, either in his own handsome home right on the banks of the Big Hole or in a nearby cabin. The Wrights moved here from Aspen a few years ago, after that popular ski village grew too popular, too crowded. Wise River has barely two hundred inhabitants, widely scattered. With help from a Bozeman architect, Phil served as his own contractor and built the exquisite house with its massive brick fireplace and wide picture windows that face the river and the mountains; he and Joan lived in a trailer the first two winters, while the house was being built, and now stay year-round in Wise River. With three well-fitted rubber rafts and one McKenzie River boat, he and some excellent local guides—Gary LaFontaine, Nevin Stephenson, Glenn West—provide memorable float trips throughout the season, according to what rivers are in best condition, on such waters as the Big Hole, Beaverhead, Jefferson, Madison, and Clark's Fork. Phil has a small but well-equipped tackle shop on his premises, the Complete Fly Fisher, and his wife, Joan, prepares not only gourmet breakfasts and dinners but superb lunches for each float.

Doug Swisher had come over from Darby, where his casting school was based, for a few days and had promptly taken a nineteen-inch rainbow on a Matuka streamer, not a hundred yards from Phil's back porch. We had floated together the first day, in two boats, along with Bill Locke. I had learned a lot. To fish with Phil is not merely to float down a river but to be instructed with great skill. In fact, Phil has a little pond close to his home, fitted with a casting platform, and likes to check out a client's casting before even starting a float. I had wanted to rush out quickly that first day after I landed in Butte, to be on the water fishing, but Phil had insisted that a half hour on his casting platform would pay dividends: this was a different kind of fishing and would require special casts. He was right, and he is a splendid instructor. Under his patient guidance, I improved my curve casts, tightened my loop, learned the double haul and the importance of line-hand control. Combined with Phil's sure sense of where the fish would be and how best to cast for them, my improved casting paid off. My casts were stronger and surer, they were better placed, I kept better control of the line after the fly hit the water, and I had learned to fish the lethal white Marabou Muddler with its shiny tinsel chenille body.

We had taken some good fish those first few days: graylings (which I had never caught before), high-jumping rainbows in fast water, bright wild browns, and whitefish (which everyone here called "Big Hole salmon"). We had floated through slate-gray canyons, along the base of buttes and sharp rock outcroppings, and through the broad umber fields of the upper Big Hole Valley, where hay was piled like gigantic loaves of baked bread, the scattered stands of aspen were dull yellow and pink on the slopes, and the pungent odor of mint along the banks was so strong you could smell it midriver. I had drunk in the tan hills, merging into one another, spotted with the dark green of lodgepole pine and Englemann spruce and Douglas fir; I had watched formations of geese push past us on a float, and I had seen cottontails and beaver, muskrat and mink and white-tailed deer. I thought I saw pheasants rise in the fields, but Phil laughed when I pointed to them and said they were only magpies, which the ranchers call "Holstein pheasants." There was dusty pink Indian paintbrush along the banks, bush cinquefoil, rabbit brush, tall orange tansy, beige buckwheat. A week ago I would not have known their names.

We ate Joan's picnic lunches on spits of land along the shore: buffalo salami, lamb sandwiches, deviled eggs, cold quiche with fine herbs from her garden, French cheeses, dried apricots, chewy nuggets, and dry white wine. Always there was a handy pot of Wright's Gorp—a mixture of walnuts, M&Ms, raisins, and other nuts and chocolate—to provide instant energy. And on one perfectly freezing float late one afternoon, we dipped into Joan's lunch box and found a thermos of broth, bouillon, and sherry, a mixture of the gods and surely better than any Saint Bernard for instant aid. Once, when I could not tear myself from the river at lunchtime, Phil brought me a glass of chilled wine while I fished, and nothing ever tasted better—nor was I ever in a finer dining spot, not in Paris or New York—and I gave him the rod and watched and sipped.

But mostly I loved the river. It had not given itself up easily; it had demanded much of me. If I did not fish it deftly, it withheld its charms. Five inches to the right or left—even less—mattered greatly. It was better, as B.O.D.E. knew, when a river gave up its bounty hard, when you had to concentrate with every ounce of your intensity to move a fish, when the fish were wild and wary and fought hard when you had been good enough to hook them. You knew they were there, many of them, and of good size, but you also knew that none of them could come easy. It was never like finding a stretch of hatchery fish on an Eastern river and catching them by the wagonful. Each fish was his own picky, individual self. Each had to be teased with the nicest care.

Doug, a dazzling fisherman, did extremely well that first day, casting left-handed or right-handed, as the situation demanded, attacking the river: two big rainbows on a green Matuka, a batch of smaller rainbows and a fifteen-inch grayling on an Adams when a caddis hatch started. And the next day he took a fine brown on a Matuka and several others on his own tie for a floating caddis pupa. I did best, at first, on Bodmer's Colorado King and Phil's own tie, the Wright's Royal, a general terrestrial imitation. We returned the fish we caught; Phil pushes catch-and-release, and we do so anyway.

On that third day, floating with Bill Locke and Phil, I had learned the short hard cast into the pockets. "Isn't that too hard?" I asked Phil as he slapped the large Marabou Muddler hard against the bank, stripped it back a few feet, then quickly cast hard again.

"No," he said. "It seems to provoke or intimidate them in their homes. We call it the Intruder Theory. The fish suddenly see this big thing streak through *their* territory and it apparently maddens them. They'll come charging up at it. You'll never see harder strikes."

And I didn't.

I had three or four lunging strikes that day—when good browns busted up from behind a rock and charged the fly with a fine fury—and several days later, on the Beaverhead, I took some fine trout, using this method. It was one of many new techniques I learned for Western fly-fishing.

II

On the far side of the heavy main current, in a flat backwater pool, I saw the fish rise. A good trout? Perhaps. You could not tell for sure, not at this distance: the pool was more than a hundred feet away. The autumn afternoon was bright and the pool was flat, so you could see the widening circle clearly enough, but you could not fish for the trout from where I stood. The main current was heavy and deep, with rolling whitecaps a foot high, impossible to wade; the cast was far too long.

I fished slowly upstream until I was opposite the backwater pool and could see it better. A small channel came in out of the woods, or perhaps it was a feeder creek from the sloping sagebrush hills; it hit up against a huge slate-gray boulder— twelve feet high, the size of a trapper's cabin—pinched into a riffle, met a channel from the main current, swirled, flattened out, became glassy, and washed slowly over some small rocks into the main river. Fish could come into the pool either from the feeder or from the main current. There would be ample food and cover—the depth beneath the rock would have to be eight to ten feet. I ached to fish the spot but there was no way I could reach it. The main current, for as far as I could see down and upstream, was too heavy, the depth too great; I could not do it, and it was impossible to cast across the broad current, then the small spit of rocks, into that pool. It was much too far. And even if I could reach it with a cast, the main current was so surging and powerful that it would tear the fly away in an instant when the line hit the water.

So I kept working my way carefully up my side of the river,

which was quite safe and easy, first fishing a caddis fly into the slack eddies directly upstream, then casting a large Marabou Muddler directly across and into the heaviest flow and, as it swung below me, working it back with short, sharp strips.

Nothing. Not even a follow.

I had not seen a fish in two hours of hard fishing. Surely this was the side everyone fished; it was not far from the road—in fact, it was a run named after a famous writer. *Everyone* fishing this river would have made a pilgrimage to this spot, to fish where that man had fished; I had done exactly that. If there were trout on this side, they would be wary, jaded, used; there probably were not many of them. And I did not particularly want to fish where everyone else had fished. I had not come all this distance to do so. I had come from that crowded place, where I always felt myself pinched and torn and manipulated. I had tried to save a few fresh places in myself, somewhere. I tried often to smile there— until my cheeks ached—but I laughed less there lately. I often felt there as if puppet strings were attached to my limbs—and soul. You could not see them but they were there. Here, the mornings at the old cabin, one of the oldest in the valley, had been so cold they sparked your face, and at the main house there had been good food, long hours of pleasant talk, and enough Scotch. But I had not come for that. I had come to be on the river. To be away. Alone. It was only for a short time. I knew that. I knew I would have to go back. But I did not have to think about that, not yet.

I had left the small party of men that morning and gone off by myself. I had liked being with them all. They were easy to be with, each of them; I liked to talk to them and I had learned from them. I had looked closely at each of them: they were younger and older men, and you knew who they were and that they knew where they were going. I was in the middle of things, not sure which way, of many, I should turn.

I was upstream of the backwater pool now. Oh, it was a perfectly marvelous pool; you might have painted it, although it was almost too pretty—wild, untouched, picturesque. There were three or four yellowed cottonwoods on the far bank, a bright yellow and pink aspen, a jam of gray weathered logs and deadfalls above the big rock. The feeder creek was bright auburn in the sun, and it sliced through a tunnel of overhanging willows, which were also spotted with yellow. I could see several of the dusty pink flowers of Indian paintbrush, and beige rabbit brush along the far shore.

The fish rose again, at the tail of the little foam line, where the riffle widened, bubbled, and flattened out. Had anyone fished that pool? Ever? It was late September and the river was low, probably as low as it ever got, and you could not cross it; in the spring and early summer the main current must have been a torrent. The high sagebrush hills were backed up close to the far bank, and there were no bridges for ten miles in either direction. Floaters might have paused there, on the long spit of land; yes, a good guide would have brought a boat up below the pool, on the far side. It was probably not virgin. You could not expect that any more, hardly anywhere. Not even in Montana. But certainly it was less fished.

That circle formed again in the middle of the pool. It spread, then vanished.

I waded steadily upstream now, my fly stuck around the brace of the lowest guide. Above me the river was turning in a broad, sweeping bend before it drew itself tighter, dropped, and swept heavily for at least a mile downstream. In the middle of the bend I saw a patch of lighter, shallower water.

The river was a hundred and twenty feet across here; the water was heavy, perhaps deeper than my waist at all times. Should I try it? Upstream I could see a series of long, deep pools, separated by short, heavy runs. If I were to cross, it would have to be here.

I studied the water. Was it possible? If it simply could not be done, I did not want to try. I could not see the entire riverbed. A pothole, a slip, a fall in such water—I did not want to think of what would happen. Footloose, there was little way a wader could regain footing; he would be swept, tumbling, into heavy water, several hundred yards of white water without a break. That would do the damage, all right. And for what? That pool was a pretty little place, and it held at least one feeding trout. Was that enough? There were other days, other portions of this river to fish.

I had already caught some good fish on this trip and knew I would catch more. I was not hungry. That first day I had been frantic to catch some fish; it was cleansing to do so. But today I could pass up that pool. Perhaps the water would drop a few more inches and I could fish it later in the week. And if I did not? Perhaps the next time I came out here I could get across. I would surely come here again and the pool would always be there.

But I felt drawn to it. I did not know what it contained and would never know until I had laid a fly on its surface. It was there.

Yes, I'd try.

I checked that my fly was secure and then shuffled slowly into the heavier current. I felt it tug and bend my legs. My cleated felt soles would hold the bottom, but I wished I had cut a thick willow branch for a staff. I leaned upstream into the flow and nudged forward. Each time I lifted my foot away from the firm riverbed, the water caught and forced it downstream. I shuffled. I saw an old aspen on the opposite bank, ten yards upstream, and headed for that. The water came up to my waist, then an inch higher. The flow was growing heavier with each step I took closer to the center. I shuffled another foot, two feet farther, then stopped. I wanted to turn around, to see how far I had come, how far I would have to return if this venture proved impossible. But I could not turn my body, only my head, and that not far. I realized, suddenly, with a spur of fear, that the current was now too heavy for me to risk turning. I was balanced sideways against the current; I was quite sure, if I faced my body flush upstream or down even for a moment, even with the good grip my cleated soles had in the riverbed, even if I summoned all my strength, that the force of the current would spill me. I knew it would happen. I could feel the river's power when I turned even slightly. It was like holding a plank of pine in the water: if you faced the thin edge to the current, it held; if you turned the wide part upstream, the current kicked it high and you could not possibly hold the bottom no matter how hard you tried. If I wanted to head back toward the safe side of the river, I would have to back out inch by inch, with the chance of bumping some unseen rock and losing control. I had been able to get out from the safe side, but unless I found the exact same way back I might not be able to return.

I held my position for a moment. The water was crystalline but deceptive. It seemed to hold at its present depth but I could not be sure. I bent carefully at the waist to check more carefully—and almost lost my balance.

"Careful. Very steady, old boy. Steady now," I said audibly. They were the first words I had spoken in several hours. They sounded hoarse, alien.

"I'd be dead without the cleats and felt."

I shuffled a bit farther. The water was at the tip of my vest now; I felt its surging, forceful rhythms against my whole body. My foot bumped a rock, felt left, then right. I raised my foot ever so gently, trying to get above the rock—teetered wildly for a moment—then scratched it across.

"I'm not going to make it. It's too strong."

I had fully half the river to cross, perhaps a trifle less. I could not turn back and was terrified of pushing even one foot ahead. "It's not possible." My palm, where I held my rod, was slippery. My face was drenched. A couple of caddis flies danced on the bright surface. The sun was strong on my neck and wrists and on the water. The aspen on the far bank did not seem much closer. I did not look toward the sky.

I tried to conjure a picture of the pool but could not. I had words for it now—I could have described it—but I could not see it clearly. I knew only that I wanted to fish it. Fishing that pool was all that mattered to me; it was a thing I was determined to do. I might catch nothing, I might never tell anyone of this fling, I might catch merely a whitefish or a chub, but I was going to fish that pool.

Methodically, ever so slowly, I inched closer to the aspen. Half a foot at a time. The soles of my waders merely pushing along the riverbed. A pause. The grating scratch of my cleats against a mossy rock the size of a grapefruit. Water high above my waist now. Two inches from the top of my waders. A slight depression. Tiptoes! The cold spurt of icy water slipping past my stomach into my trousers. Slowly. Very slowly. A minute, two minutes for each couple of inches. Scratch and nudge and tiny shuffle.

And then I felt the slight waning of the current pressure against my body, watched the water line drop two inches, four, felt my step grow surer, and bolted—splashing, high-stepping—the last five yards to the shore.

I breathed heavily and felt my entire body soften. I felt the rowel of pain in my arches and the biting sting in my right shoulder, merely from holding my rod high. I kept breathing heavily, panting, smiling broadly to myself, and then, without waiting to calm down, I half ran, half tumbled through the stand of cottonwood and aspen to the pool.

When I got down to the end of the woods, I stood for a moment looking at my pool. There was no hurry now. I had spent more than an hour getting to this place, and I did not want to spoil it.

What I had thought was a feeder was really a back channel of the main river. The hole was far deeper than I had guessed. Where it hit against the rock, it was so deep you could not see the bottom; angles and fractured planes of light descended toward the point of a cone and disappeared. One had to imagine what lay in the depths. The water might have cut under the rock a full ten feet. Big trout, really big trout, could live under there for a lifetime, having all their food washed down to them, being perfectly safe from all manner of predators. You could not work a fly under that rock; it went back too far, the current was too rough. You would even have trouble working bait back down into the recesses of that hole. Whatever lay down there was safe. There was no honorable way to take a fish that lived there.

Perhaps, though, one of them would come into the pool at times, take a position where the foam line of the current grew lazy, and pluck some hatching fly from the surface. It would not have to, any more than I had to cross over to this far side of the river—for there was surely enough food at the bottom of the hole—but it might, some day, for some reason.

There were tangled currents at the head of the pool where the two channels met; one might find trout there, too, not five feet from where I stood. But the glare of the sun was strong; they had no protection but the broken water. Any really large fish would surely be on the far side, near or under that boulder, in deeper water.

I was still breathing heavily as I watched the pool. I leaned my rod into some low willows, took off my hat, and scooped some water from the main current onto my face. Nothing could have felt finer. There was plenty of time. I had gotten to this pool. I saw some deer tracks in the mud, rabbit droppings along the rocks. I saw how the water broke ever so slightly, down where the foam line widened, not in a rise but perhaps a bulge. I measured with my eye the kind of cast I would have to make to reach it. Forty feet downstream, perhaps, but with slack enough so that it would not drag too soon. And I would have to cast over the tangled currents. I could do that. The alley of the channel would support my back cast, and I could probably stop the rod short enough to lay down five feet of slack line.

But the better cast, surely, would be from *below* the rock—a short upstream cast, over flat water. That would take another fifteen minutes.

I had come this far, I thought, why not do it right?

I walked a short way up the shallow channel, crossed to the base of the hill, and walked down toward the rock. Those deadfalls and weathered logs were jammed high, from some spring freshet, and I had to climb through and over them, then under a huge fallen pine whose stubby branches caught my vest. The trek took a good while, and I was sweating again when I stood on the rock bed below the pool, in exactly the right position. I was precisely where I wanted to be.

I watched the water closely for five minutes. I had been careful, but perhaps the noise or my shadow had spooked the fish. There was no hurry, no hurry at all. A few small tan caddis danced on the surface. A magpie fluttered noisily out of the cottonwoods. The sky was bright cobalt, flecked with white. Then, suddenly, a fish rose at the end of the foam line.

The water was so clear and open that I feared I would get only one or two casts here. I wanted to cast at once but I stepped back a few feet, sat on a rock, and clipped off the No. 12 caddis I had been using. I took out my pipe, packed it slowly with tobacco, and puffed deeply. Then I tied on a length of 5X tippet, tested it, and fetched out a No. 18 tan caddis. I pulled the tippet through a patch of rubber I carried to straighten it, then ran it through my mouth to help it sink quickly.

"Now," I said. "Now."

I drew eight or ten lengths of line from my reel slowly, so the click was muffled. I false-cast across the stream three or four times, then swiveled slightly and cast two feet upstream and somewhat to the side of where the fish had risen.

The fly floated several inches, swirled languidly in a pinch of the current, came out of the little eddy, floated another inch, then another . . . slowly, now—and the fish took.

If I fish another forty years I will never forget the quick little splash, the spurt of water, the circle forming on that glassy, silent pool; nor the speed with which my rod hand raised firmly and hooked the fish; nor the sight of its three hard jumps, smashing the stillness.

It was a bright male brown, about fourteen inches—wild, brilliantly spotted, quite plump. It had never seen a fly. In a few minutes I slipped the hook out of its jaw and turned it free.

Later, my friends asked me what luck I'd had. "No luck," I said, laughing. "But I managed to take one fish, on the far side of the river."

"How big?" one of them asked.

"Not very," I said. "But sweet. Very sweet."

III

Three men about my age, from Iowa, came into the shop, looked at the register, and said, "Good heavens! Nick Lyons has been here."

I wasn't sure whether that was good or bad—since I am too well known for bringing monstrous luck wherever I go (hurricanes to Martha's Vineyard, torrential rains to the Beaverkill). It certainly was not the same as George Washington, Ernest Schwiebert, or Kilroy's having been there. But they seemed like kindly folk, not superstitious, and had already mentioned that they had had good luck, so I took a chance and said, "Yes, and he's still here."

"*You're* Nick Lyons?" they said, almost in unison. And then, in unison, went silent and scrutinized me. Then one of them said—did I detect a touch of reverence?—"You are the master of frustration!"

"Sure, you speak for all of us," said another. "For the poor guy who sits in his office all year dreaming, gets out for only two weeks a year, and then bungles everything."

Was it true?

Perhaps.

Next to Sparse, who lets us know in *Fishless Days, Angling Nights*, quite modestly, about only two small trout he caught—but whom everyone knows to be a man who simply does not bother with smaller than fifty-pound Scotch-guzzling browns—I have probably written more about *not* catching fish—about getting hooks in my ear, falling in, nearly losing my prized equipment and lovely wife—than anyone else, ever. It is not a distinction I particularly sought.

It is not a distinction that B.O.D.E. would have cherished. I would much rather be known as the first man to cast three hundred feet backhanded or to take a ten-pound brown from the Blue Kill on a No. 24 Blue Spinner. But in what I have seen of my future, those things are not in it.

As I thought about it, I cringed to think that about the only three people in Iowa who knew me, knew me for my blunders. I half expected them to ask not how many trophy fish I had caught but which guides I had hooked in the nose with a Marabou Muddler. In fact, I thought I saw one of them looking closely at Phil's left ear.

The truth, though, was that I was not in the least frustrated and had had a minimum number of disasters that week. None worth talking about. Actually I felt positively gleeful about a couple of dazzling casts I had made that very afternoon—they would have knocked your eye out. But then I worried. If I got really good—I mean, like the experts— would I have anything to write about? What could I say then? I caught ninety-three trout in two hours? Rumor has it that George LaBranche gave up trout fishing because he no longer found it a challenge. Would I ever come to the same sad end? Well, I wasn't going to get *that* good, not ever.

I found myself mumbling, trying to avoid bragging about several good fish I had moved. I really wanted to tell them about that, but they kept quoting my disasters to me. Had I really exposed my secret fumbling life so well? Didn't I know it all already, to my great shame? Still, the disasters *were* rather amusing and fun to tell, and true—how true!—and it would have been downright boastful of me to mention that I had taken, oh, five or six decent fish that very day. There didn't seem much point to such a story.

After they left, I was on the verge of asking Phil if he knew some brushy irrigation ditch where I might catch some funny disasters, when I thought, boldly, No. I am going to play this straight. I am getting unbelievably good and there is no truth in downplaying it any longer, letting misconceptions gather in Iowa. I will have to start admitting to my success even if it spoils my reputation forever.

So I promptly asked Phil whether, if I gave up the city and all its exotic pleasures, he could make a steely-eyed Montana guide out of me. To my shock he said he could and later even sent me a guide's application. But he told me that guiding could get flaky at times: all that rowing, watching other guys catch fish. He told me about one sport who would not keep the line over his finger and threw tremendous slack. The fly kept whizzing around Phil's head—and finally stuck him. "Look," Phil had to say, "we're doing this my way from now on or we're not doing it at all." Whereupon, he said, "Watch," took the rod, and, keeping one hand on the oars, cast close up to the bank, controlled the line with his line-hand finger, got lucky, and *bam!* a good trout hit.

That did not seem too frustrating to me. I'd take a fly in the neck any day for a chance to perform like that, in front of such an audience

"Then there's the Mrs. Flannagan Problem," he said.

"Is that bad?"

"The worst."

"Frustrating?"

"Immensely so. I was floating with two men one day, catching absolutely zilch, when we turned a bend and saw a woman with a marvelously shapely rump, bent over in the fish-catching position."

"That doesn't sound frustrating," I said.

"It is when you're a high-priced Montana guide, doing not a thing for your clients that day. She caught two while we floated toward her. I had to decide quickly whether to row like mad and get through the run as fast as possible or stop and see if we could do something. By the time we stopped on the opposite bank she'd caught two more; her own husband—who I recognized as Mr. Flannagan—was getting furious himself, since she was catching fish faster than he could clean them. The situation was increasingly embarrassing, especially since none of us could keep our eyes off her shapely rump, and the men didn't want to move downstream."

I tried some rowing the next day and was not frustrated by it at all. In fact, I once tried to grab the rod from Phil when he made a cast perhaps two inches too short, but he held on to it stubbornly.

Then Phil said that maybe I ought to get a dose of the way guides live, so he let me sleep in the guides' shack, which had no heat or running water. It was terrific. I never slept better. No more posh accommodations for me, ever; all I needed was an old trapper's shack, an old spring mattress, some sturdy grub, and your strongest bourbon. In the morning I felt like galloping across the frosty field and bathing in the icy Big Hole.

After all this Montana fishing I really had to resign my title. It didn't fit any more. I was too steely-eyed, impervious to pain, deft. I was ready to buy myself a leather guide's hat that day and a beige chamois shirt.

I began to think of how, when I got back home, I was sure to rant and rave about all the fish I had caught, how my prowess was becoming legendary west of the Continental Divide, how we should sell everything and *all* become guides, a tribe of them. But then one of my wiseacre kids would surely ask if I had any pictures of all those legendary trout, and I would have to tell him honestly, "Well, I put the first roll of film in backward and ripped the second."

"You didn't catch any!" one of them would say.

"I really did. Dozens. Big fish. Very big fish. And I got some good shots of them on the third roll."

"So?"

"Well, you see, I tripped getting out of the rubber raft, wrenched my ankle, burned my wrist with my cigar, ripped my waders, the cleats of which were tangled in the coils of my fly line, ruining it, and the camera . . ."

"Same old Dad," they would say in unison—and yawn.

IV

Nick Adams, in B.O.D.E.'s story "Now I Lay Me," is afraid that if he shuts his eyes in the dark his soul will go out of his body. He is in Italy, during World War I, and he keeps himself together and awake by thinking of trout streams he has fished when he was a boy. He fishes the whole length of each of them, very carefully and very patiently in his mind. Sometimes he concocts streams and gives them each a name and local habitation, and in time these mingle with real ones, confused with rivers he really fished.

All night, closing my eyes tightly, I have been trying to recapture an afternoon so real, so precious to me, I want never to forget a moment of it. All night I have been rebuilding in my mind the afternoon, the particular stretch of the river I fished. I remember the facts easily enough, the number of fish I caught and how, but the picture, the image, the colors, the feel of it keep slipping away already, mingling with the sensations of other trips, merging, even tonight; then, abruptly, a touch of it returns, the strike of that rainbow, the shape of those tangled branches where the huge one rose, the big brown hovering in the clear water near my boots, the fly loosely in its mouth.

The morning had been slow and we had split up after

lunch and I had gone upstream with Nevin, the burly mous-
tached guide from Butte who for an hour had told me of the
four- and five-pounders this river still produced. "It's not an
easy river," he said, "and sometimes you think they're not
there. But when it comes alive—watch out!"

I had seen nothing of size. I had heard that the farmers
took too much water for irrigation and bulldozed the spawn-
ing beds; I had heard that the great days of this river were
over, merely legend now. It was useless to dream otherwise.
So my expectations were low as we came shuffling in our
chest-high waders through the woods from the road, crossing
old gray buckrail fences and following the narrow dirt path
through stands of yellowed cottonwoods. I saw grasshoppers
in the high autumn grasses—tan and charcoal and beige—
and could hear them crisply flopping among the fallen
leaves. Through the trees I could see layers of mountain
ranges, turning from purple to light gray, some laced with a
filigree of low clouds, some spotted already with snow. The
morning, like every other morning all week, had been
sharply chill and very bright; now it was warmer, so you did
not notice the weather and how pleasant it was until you
thought about it, and there were no strong breezes and the
lazy clouds only occasionally shielded the sun.

Nevin took me to a run that was fast and deep, perhaps
seventy feet across, more than a hundred yards long. You
had to wade deep, over your waist, to get enough room for a
proper back cast, to reach the opposite bank. The water came
strong against the far bank, which was bowed and copper-
colored and hard dried mud; the grassy sod at the top, maybe
three feet from the surface of the water, protruded like a
peaked cap. There was a rim of slower, eddying water, not
four inches wide, along the bank, and you knew that was
where the fish were.

I did not particularly want company that afternoon—even

Nevin's, which was good—so I told him to fish, not guide, and after pointing out to me the whereabouts of some likely runs upriver, he began to cast a big Marabou Muddler downstream at the tail of the run. I got in above him and began to fish up. I wanted a big fly, something worth the while of the big trout that would be in the eddies and slack water, even under the banks along the far side; I wanted something that would tease them, tempt them, draw them out. The grasshopper would do just fine.

We had been floating the day before, and though I had been caught up in the special excitement of quick runs through a vast variety of new water, I welcomed the chance to wade and stalk. When you floated, you got one cast, maybe two at a likely pocket, then shot downstream and had to find another. You moved so fast it seemed the water was shooting upstream past you. Now I could move slowly, prepare my cast, pick my position and target with care. Now I could choose my fly for a particular spot and change it without having to worry that I would have to change it again, and miss choice water, while the raft swept downriver. I felt more in control. I felt that whatever results I had would be more my own doing. Now the water was clearly flowing down and past me; now the woods, as they should be, were rooted.

I waded deep and cast across to the opposite bank. The hopper splatted down and floated like a little orange twig, bounced with the riffles, and went under after it dragged a few inches. I took nothing on five or six casts and saw no fish working. Perhaps my fly was too far out. It ought to be right up against that bank, no more than inches from it. I cast again, hitting the mudbank, shaking out a foot of slack line quickly. That was better. That was the kind of cast I needed. I hit the little curve in the bank again and then again. Nothing. I moved a few feet upstream and directed my cast a bit more sharply upstream to give my fly a better float. Still better. Three more casts, four.

There was a spurt of water just before the fly went under. A good fish. It had chased the fly; it had come out from the slack water near the bank and lunged at the fly but it had missed.

I remember how my body grew alive at the sight of that first rise, how every part of me awoke. There were good fish in this run, and I had a fly that would tempt them and another eighty yards of the run still to fish, right up to that tangle of deadfalls, where the river pinched and bent and rushed in against the bank.

I shuffled another few feet upstream, watching the line where the surface of the water met the opposite bank. The long, gnarled roots of an aspen dropped through the sod peak and were exposed, and the bank upstream of them had been eroded by spring freshets. There was a slight declivity, of perhaps two feet, where the water backed up after it hit the roots. It was not an easy cast, but I found with my eye the spot on the bank I would have to hit if the fly was to reach that little eddy on a free float, cast, hit it, tensed, leaned forward as the fly began its drift, reached my rod forward still more to get another few inches of float, saw it hit the eddy, swirl, and begin to pull out.

And then the rainbow struck, quite savagely, sending a spurt of water high.

I raised my rod, felt the fish, and watched the iridescent thing jump four times in rapid succession, then make the mistake of boring upstream, where it would be sure to tire itself against the rush of the heavy current. In five minutes I had it in close, slipped the big hopper hook out, and watched the fish dart away.

A good fish. A very good fish, perhaps seventeen inches. And fat, at least two pounds.

I checked the fly, dipped it in the water, sprayed it again with flotant, and shuffled a bit farther upstream. I had gotten one good fish; that made the afternoon already. I never needed a lot of fish, only a few good well-earned fish, to make a day. This one had only come when I had cast just right. I'd had to stalk it; I'd had to place the fly perfectly or the fish would not have been able to see it or get at it.

I took another two trout along that bank—good, firm, wild fish—as I worked my way upstream, wading deep, watching the jagged line where the river met the undercut bank, feeling myself grow more and more deeply into the world of this Montana river. Its sound was in my head now, rushing, filling me; I was enclosed within the alley of the stream, melting into it, part of it; I saw only the river's writhing swiftness and the blaze of brightness when a fish took. None came easily. When my cast was short, no fish showed. When my float was too brief, I got nothing. This was blind stalking of a very particular brand: you could not see the fish; they were deep and they were not regularly rising to any natural insects. You had to fish where you thought they would be, fish the water rather than any rise. They were deep and they hugged the far bank but they could be pounded up. They would come up for the big grasshopper imitation; it was large enough to coax them up out of their lies, if your cast was exactly where it should be.

At the head of the run, where the river pinched, shot into a massive tangle of deadfalls, and squeezed out in a rush between the thin tips of many branches, I stopped, took out a cigar, and watched the water. I had taken an hour and a half, perhaps two hours, to fish that short run; I had worked very hard for the four fish I had caught. In the branches there were several large wet flies and one streamer, along with four or five spinning lures, with their tails of curled monofilament. Deep under those three square yards of fallen trees, there would surely be big trout, and these trout would be so well protected that even the most cunning fisherman could not take them. They had cover, and they would get plenty of food without moving from their sanctuary. You could not fish for them from above, not even with bait: the water was too heavy, the tangles too thick and complex. In the early season, when the water was high, no doubt covering many of the deadfalls, fishermen would cast streamers and lures into that maze and lose them, or the lures would swing in the current high above the fish. Only now, perhaps, when the water was low, would a large *dry* fly, well cast and floating high and safely around some of the branches, lure some of them out.

I studied the maze for five minutes. You could perhaps lure a fish up once, perhaps twice, out of tangles such as those. No more. Your cast would have to go upstream at a sharp angle, right into the crotch of that wishbone configuration of branches near the far bank; you'd have to shake out a foot of slack immediately, give the fly a dramatic twitch or two at once, to make a fish commit itself before the fly came out of the eddying water and into the heavy head of current. Then, if you were lucky, very lucky, the fish would come several feet downstream, out of the tangles, and you would have a chance.

It was a slim chance.

But I was feeling very good about myself and I was feeling very lucky. I had taken four nice fish in fast water and still had a long afternoon ahead of me, with several runs already in sight above the bend. Nevin had even said those would be best.

My first cast, miraculously, was within two inches of the point of the wishbone. I rolled out a foot of slack, watched the fly swivel and do a jig in the tangled currents, and saw, suddenly—my heart slipping into my kidneys—a gigantic circle the size of a sink form behind the fly just as it hit the forward current and shot out of the pocket.

What an awesome rise!

That fish could have been five, ten, perhaps even fifteen pounds. They had come out of this river that size—not many, not often any more, but sometimes, some of them.

I cast again, far too quickly this time, hung my fly on the near branch and had to add it to the Christmas decorations. Then I cast again, again clumsily, and lost another fly. Two more casts. Ten more. Twenty. More slowly, less hopefully at the end. Nothing.

Upstream, about an hour later, I found a split in the river, where two channels came down from sharply diverging directions, making an island. I could cross the shallow riffles here, and I chose the far channel, which probably could not be fished earlier in the season. It was a picture-book run. The water entered in a sprightly rush of white water no more than fifteen feet across, then widened and slowed, flowing under some overhanging willows in a large bow bend for some sixty yards. The water was quite clear here and I could see the deep slope of the riverbed, perhaps ten feet in the center. Along the far bank there was a steady foam line; the line was some four or five inches from the bank, mostly, a snaking line that grew thin, then widened, then thinned out again, then swirled as it hit against the bank here and there, and turned out again. It was clearly a feeding lane. I looked but could see no fish in the deep center trench; they would be up along the far bank, under the willows, close enough to that feeding lane so they could see whatever came down in the foam or in the midwater current.

I was in no hurry.

I had caught several more fish, none under fourteen inches. I had raised that one really good fish in the wishbone tangles and had had four or five other good follows.

The water was so slow and clear here that I changed to a better hopper imitation: Dave's Hopper, which has no extraneous hackle, a sharper silhouette, and a lower profile on the water. I changed, too, to a lighter leader, 5X. I'd stay with a Hopper; it had been my first fly of the day and had taken all my fish. There were some caddis dancing on the surface and some stone-fly cases on the dull-pewter rocks, but you stay with what is working until it does not work any more. Later, perhaps, I would try the small elk-hair caddis that had worked so well the day before.

There was time to be leisurely, slow. I sat on the trunk of a fallen tree, at a spot nearly at the bow of the bend, where I could watch the entire run, upstream and down. I saw deer tracks in the bleached sand near my feet and looked out over the expanse of mountains. Arching branches etched their design against the blaze of blue. There were patches of fields the color of old leather and silvered buckrail fences, long unused. How little I had seen of country like this these past twenty years; how much I had dreamed of such a day! It was here and I was in it and I did not want to lose one twig or riffle. I wanted to remember every detail of this secluded channel: the scurry of several hares in the underbrush; the abrupt flutter of magpies; the gigantic sky; the particular blush pink of the aspens and yellow of the cottonwoods, not yellow like any other yellow but cottonwood-yellow of a particular day and place; the simple sounds of the light wind and moving water; and the lazy twist and turn of the foam line as it formed at the head of the channel and threaded its way down, skirting the far bank, under the half-fallen aspen, to the tail of the run below me. I was a long way from that place where one could comfortably lose himself in the elusive fiction of busyness. A very long distance.

Did it matter any more if I caught another fish or not? Not really. I had taken six and I had missed a really good one. I had had a fine day of it and one fish more or less did not matter. I knew I should walk back to the tail of the pool and fish up slowly. I would not have to wade—the channel was not that wide; I could reach the far bank comfortably without having to muss the water. I should fish the hopper or perhaps an elk-hair caddis, up every foot of this channel, right against the bank, in and beyond the foam line. There had to be fish there, and if I fished carefully I knew I could take four or five of them without spoiling the water.

"Drowsèd with the fume of poppies," Keats says in his poem "To Autumn," this season of mellow fruitfulness can spare "the next swath and all its twined flowers." I too was drowsed and could spare this channel. I had none of the taut, keen hunter left in me; I did not have to compete or prove or test or even try. I felt beyond escape. It was so peaceful just sitting there, eyes alive and awake, letting all come to me, sure that what did come was fruitful and true. I did not have to protect eye and ear from all that grates and encroaches. My blinders were off. Every secret part of me was unlocked.

But would just a few casts spoil the moment? Not hardly. Not ever.

So I got up off the log and walked slowly to a spot where I could cast to one particular crook in the channel that I had been watching, where the bank was indented several feet and the foam line entered the eddy, swirled, twisted, and somehow found its downstream course again. I wanted to cast several feet above that eddy, get my fly into the foam line, let it swirl down into that pocket.

It was a short cast, less than thirty feet, and I managed it well the first time. The fly came down, turning gently, slipped into the pocket, and I twitched it twice, and the surface broke in a sharp little gash of silver. I struck and knew at once that I was into the biggest fish of the day.

The fish bore deeply along the far bank, downstream, and with the delicate leader I lowered my rod and let it take line from the reel. Downstream it went, slowly, heavily, then with a rush. Along the bank, stumbling as I went, I moved down with it, keeping the line gently taut. This was a good fish, and after being indifferent to fishing I suddenly wanted to see it, to bring it to shore.

The line angled toward the surface and I felt sure the fish was going to jump. But it merely swirled, heavily, and bore deep again. There were few obstructions in the run, and there was too little current to be of much help to the fish. It was tiring. Its runs were shorter but still threatening. Closer. A little nearer and I would be able to see it. There. A brown. A really big brown—over twenty inches. A male, brightly colored, its jaw slightly hooked. I could see it, deep in the clear water, struggling, head down and away from me, against the tug of my line.

And then the fish was in the shallows and I had it. It was almost too beautiful to touch, hovering there in the clear water near my boots, the fly loosely in its mouth. I bent down and merely flicked the big hook of the Hopper free. For a moment the big brown—beaten but upright—did not realize it was no longer attached to me. Then it did—and vanished.

On my way downstream to the car, I took another good fish on the Hopper in fast water and then paused at the great tangle of branches. Should I fish it again? What could I do for an encore? Well, why not? I would not get back here soon. Wouldn't it be remarkable if I took the *really* big one now? So I cast three or four times up into that wishbone, but my heart was not in it and nothing rose and I was just as pleased.

I had had enough. Surfeit. The stuff that dreams are made of. Before I could tell Nevin the details, he knew; my smile was that great. For once it had been enough of a day, all I might have wanted of it—and more.

Nick Adams is afraid that if he shuts his eyes his soul will go out of his body. I am afraid that if I open them too wide— even now, before I return to the busy gray city—yesterday will vanish. I do not want it to vanish. I will not let it vanish. All night I have relived that afternoon, over and over and over.

V

The Beaverhead is a strange, deep, bushy-banked, trouty river. Norm Peterson, a local fisheries biologist who has stocked and studied the river carefully for years, told me it has one of the highest populations of trout in Montana, more than four hundred pounds per acre; he also suggested that the infamous Girdlebug—a positively ugly fly of black chenille body with rubber legs, which is used almost exclusively on the river—imitates the "green worm," crane-fly larvae that run up to two full inches in length. So curious a fly is the Girdlebug that Glenn West and I contemplated a series of them. If the standard fly worked so well, why not a *Spent* Girdlebug? An Emerging Girdlebug? Even a Stillborn Girdlebug? When I used a dropper and the two Girdlebugs came back locked together, we even contemplated Mating Girdlebugs.

The Beaverhead is a difficult river to fish, and I know many dry-fly fishermen in the East who would rather eat worms than fish it. The river is narrow and deep, lined with overhanging willows, deadfalls, tangled mazes that cover sharply undercut banks. It winds and twists so severely that at one moment you're traveling south, another north. Some sections, in the fall, are filled with heavy green weed, the edges of which invariably produce good fish.

The afternoon we checked into a motel in Dillon, the bright warm weather suddenly turned sour; there was a steady drizzle and a sharp chill that crept beneath four layers of sweaters and shirts and a parka, deep into my bones. But we were all anxious to be on the water and fishing, so we managed a four-hour float.

We used the abrupt, hard cast, as close to the shore as possible, and found fish in the crook of each big bend, and in the little pockets along the bank, under the fly-snagging deadfalls, deep in the eddies, just beyond the steady foam lines. You can't wade. You must expect to lose half a dozen flies. Little is delicate. Floating, you forget everything but that endless series of small targets against the shore. You begin to concentrate on what you cannot see, what you imagine is under water. You fish the Girdlebug on a stubby six-foot leader tapered to sixteen-pound test, almost exclusively—casting it hard into the pockets, splatting it down, flirting it in the current, teasing it through one enticing lie after the other. You know, always, that a big one, a hog, a brown that has been safely hidden in those tangles for four or five years, fat on green worms and wild and brilliantly colored, might on any cast, any time you put one of those outrageous rubber-legged monstrosities in the water, blast up, jaws open, and scare you out of your long johns.

Bill had one on that bore deep and never showed and finally pulled free; Betty Meier, who, with her husband,

Jack, fished down with us in another of Phil's boats, had one on in the current that "felt like a log." They were bright, firm, wild fish, all of them—and after I stopped pulling the fly away as a fish burst toward it, I got a batch that went about fifteen or sixteen inches those two days we floated the Beaverhead.

Then it rained hard and we returned to Phil's house and checked the Big Hole. It was high and discolored but I could not bear, being in that country for only a few more days, to miss an afternoon of fishing, despite all the good days I had had. Glenn suggested the upper Wise River, where the Wrights also lease water. It was a splendid choice. Glenn had been guiding hard all summer and fishing practically not at all; he needed an afternoon to himself, and the intimate Wise proved just the place. The water was fresh and quick, light auburn, like a cold white wine, and he and I fished it for two hours, he downstream, I up. It was a pleasant, relaxing river after the hard float-fishing we had just finished. Glenn got a fine thirteen-inch rainbow—a trophy in that water—and I took a slew of small fish that popped up in the crystalline riffles to nab my Hairwing Royal Coachman.

We had one last leisurely float on the upper Big Hole. It was a quiet day on exquisite water. We chatted and laughed and loafed and spent an hour fishing over a batch of incredibly picky seven-inch rainbows: they were taking spent *Tricorythodes*, we finally discovered, and Phil had to go down to a 7X twelve-foot leader before he hooked one. Bill, who had once rowed crew for Harvard, took the oars for a while. Phil got a chance to do something his guiding had left too little time for all summer—fishing—and Bill got a chance to do something he and I had wanted to do all week: tease and coach the steely-eyed Montana guide.

It was a sweet day, without any of the pressure hard floating demands; we caught a few fish but that was the least of it; we laughed a lot at Bill's marvelously dry New England wit, chided the guide when his cast was four inches to the left of a pocket, and ate the last of Joan's magnificent streamside lunches—after Bill said he was so hungry his stomach was beginning to wonder whether his throat had been cut.

And then it was over.

VI

After I left the Wrights the next morning I began the forty-mile drive to Butte. I was early for my plane, so I stopped on a rocky hillside overlooking a broad bend in the river. I looked down at a huge boulder, with eddies behind that *had* to hold good fish, and at the rocky pilings of an old bridge. Yellowed cottonwood and willow leaves drifted lazily in the current, and the week in all its richness flooded my thoughts: the long good talks with Bill at night, the crisp sound of frost on the ground each morning, the warm hospitality of the Wrights, the new skills I had learned and the fine water I had seen, the fish that had—in their own good time—been so generous.

I knew I would make such forays to such bright rivers again, and that I had taken so much of them inside me now that I need never worry again that I would be without them. The river that had started as an unnamed freshet, far back in the Catskills, was broader, richer, more complex now, and I had tools to fish in it and a lifetime still to fish. The circus of upper Broadway, the cold gray isolation of cities, could trouble me no more. Perhaps, like Walton, I would someday leave my London, "judging it dangerous for honest men to be there." Not yet. I took my life from another source. I had fashioned my craft to float any waters. I welcomed the work of cities. I welcomed the tangle of deadfalls in which one probed for the largest truths.

I looked at the bright river below me and thought of what Cézanne had once said: "My eyes are stuck to the point I look upon. I feel they would bleed if I tore them away."

I looked once more, deeply.

I tried to turn but could not.

Then I tore my eyes away, and found that they did not bleed, and headed home.

Prize Catches from Fireside